A LITTLE GOD TIME

FOR

MEN

BroadStreet
PUBLISHING

BroadStreet Publishing Group, LLC.
Savage, Minnesota, USA
Broadstreetpublishing.com

A Little God Time for Men
© 2022 by BroadStreet Publishing®

978-1-4245-6495-8
978-1-4245-6496-5 (eBook)

Design and typesetting by Garborg Design Works | garborgdesign.com
Editorial services by Michelle Winger | literallyprecise.com

Printed in China.

22 23 24 25 26 27 28   7 6 5 4 3 2 1

Be strong in the Lord
and in his mighty power.

EPHESIANS 6:10 NLT

INTRODUCTION

We have the incredibly important role of leading younger generations through turbulent waters, modeling integrity in relationships, and providing foundations for wise decision-making. There are times we might feel like we've got things all figured out, and other times we feel unworthy of our great responsibilities.

A Little God Time for Men is designed to help you meditate on Scripture, read thought-provoking messages, and communicate with God through prayer. It will challenge, equip, and encourage you to till the soil set before you.

Time spent with God empowers you to be a man of character, strength, and leadership. Be marked by the words written here and endeavor to be the man God has called you to be.

JANUARY

God is our refuge and strength,
Always ready to help
in times of trouble.

PSALM 46:1 NLT

PRIORITIES

*All glory to God our Father
forever and ever!*
PHILIPPIANS 4:20 NLT

The temptation we men struggle to overcome is the need for approval, affirmation, or adoration from those around us. We want love and respect from our family members, recognition from coworkers, and good standing within our community. We strive for these conditional social rewards. Something missing within us longs for acceptance, and so we shift our attention to the accolades this world so teasingly offers.

Perhaps we didn't get the approval we needed from our own fathers. Or perhaps we know we are inwardly more fragile than the lofty expectations we have placed upon ourselves. Or perhaps we are tempted to place the spotlight on ourselves. For whatever reason, if we're not proactive, our priorities can become misguided. We can be tricked into thinking, *If only others would lift me up.* It has been said that the chief end of man is to bring glory to God. The honest question that every man needs to face is this one: In all sincerity, who do I want to see glorified in my life today?

God, whenever I am swayed to seek my own stance upon your pedestal, remind me of who you are and what my priorities should be.

BLESSING

May the grace of the Lord Jesus Christ
be with your spirit.
PHILIPPIANS 4:23 NLT

At the end of his letter to his friends in the city of Philippi, Paul gave a blessing: "May the grace of the Lord Jesus Christ be with your spirit." Does anyone in your family or within your network of friends need to receive a blessing like this from you? As a man, you're in a privileged and unique situation to speak life into those who need your love. You have the incredible opportunity, through your words, to curse or to encourage those closest to you.

God wants you to extend his blessing upon others. So, today, receive the grace he has for you through Jesus and then be intentional about sharing that grace with those you love. Jesus loves you, has given his life for you, and offers you unrelenting relationship. Now do the same for others in his grace-full power.

God, may you give me more than enough grace, so I may overflow upon those around me. In the name of Jesus.

CHANGING LIVES

This same Good News that came to you is going out all over the world. It is bearing fruit everywhere by changing lives, just as it changed your lives from the day you first heard and understood the truth about God's wonderful grace.

COLOSSIANS 1:6 NLT

The good news of Jesus is that our sins are forgiven and our relationship with God is restored through his saving work on the cross. This seed, when planted, grows and bears fruit for generations.

As a man, you have a remarkable twofold calling. First, you are called to embrace the good news wherever you are, making the grace and truth of Jesus the central component of your life. Second, you are called to share this good news with anyone who comes across your path. Sow the seeds of the gospel of Jesus within their lives. Help them to cultivate their faith. Provide the water, the light, the nutrients, and the environment for their faith to flourish. And watch with joy as the good news of Jesus spreads through them. You know Jesus has impacted your life when he leads you to start impacting others. It has been said that your faith in God isn't actually yours. Rather, your faith in God is yours to give.

God, let me never cover up my faith. Continue to change my life by your Spirit and empower me to be bold in the way that I live out my commitment to you.

WORK SO HARD

We tell others about Christ, warning everyone and teaching everyone with all the wisdom God has given us. We want to present them to God, perfect in their relationship to Christ. That's why I work and struggle so hard, depending on Christ's mighty power that works within me.

COLOSSIANS 1:28-29 NLT

If you were called to a meeting with God, and if it was your special responsibility to introduce the people in your life to him, what would you say? How would you describe them to God? What would be the important aspects you would want God to know as you presented them to him? If you had your lifetime to prepare for this meeting, how would you spend your life? To what would you devote your time each day? What sorts of habits or characteristics would you hope would rub off you and onto them?

Paul tirelessly invested the qualities of his own life into others. His desire was to present people to God, perfect through Christ. He sought God's wisdom in the practice of his own faith so he would know how to teach and represent God to those he cared about. He worked so hard, not for his own gain but so others would discover and embrace the forgiveness and abundance that comes from knowing Jesus.

God, may the work of my heart and hands today be determined, strong, and courageous on behalf of those around me.

CONTINUE TO LIVE

Just as you accepted Christ Jesus as your Lord,
you must continue to follow him.
COLOSSIANS 2:6 NLT

Just because at some point in your life you committed yourself to Jesus, doesn't mean that your faith is to remain static. To be a disciple means to be a learner. In other words, a disciple of Jesus is a learner of Jesus.

Therefore, continue to follow Jesus. In fact, follow him with more attentive steps than yesterday. Learn his thoughts, learn his actions, and learn his will. Seek out his decisions for you, search out his advice, and call out for his wisdom. Run to his healing, walk where he miraculously stands, and get down into the messes in which he so willingly places himself. Embrace him as tightly today as you did at any point in your past. If Jesus is to be your Lord, let him be your Lord in every practical way today.

God, give me the resolve to continue to trust myself to your guidance, your steps, and your presence in my life. I want to follow you again today, as I did yesterday and as I will tomorrow.

DON'T GET CAUGHT

Don't let anyone capture you with empty philosophies and high-sounding nonsense that come from human thinking and from the spiritual powers of this world, rather than from Christ.

COLOSSIANS 2:8 NLT

In Genesis 3, Satan captured Adam and Eve in the Garden of Eden. He hunted them, he lured them, and then he snared them. They bought his shrewd, high-sounding nonsense. In Matthew 4, Satan tried his alluring arguments again, this time to trip up Jesus in the desert. Each statement and question lobbed by Satan was a like a high-arching softball grenade. If Jesus had taken the bait, the consequences would have been explosive. But he stayed the course. He didn't let the evil one capture him with falsehoods. In fact, he freely dispatched Satan's empty philosophies by being even shrewder than the snake.

How did he resist while Adam and Eve had fallen? What was Jesus' weapon? It was the uncompromising ballistic missile of truth. Staying alert and on course isn't just for your sake. The arguments you buy and the conclusions you accept impact the generations that follow you. Your kids will likely mimic your thoughts. Your grandchildren will likely reflect their grandfather's beliefs. If you get lost, it's likely that they will as well.

God, as for me and my family, we will serve you. Help me, then, to stay true, for the sake of those around me.

NEW NATURE

Put on your new nature, and be renewed
as you learn to know your Creator and become like him.
COLOSSIANS 3:10 NLT

In Genesis 1, God merely spoke, and the stars were born. He said, "Let there be…" and there was. In the beginning, Christ was the Word (mentioned in John 1) who declared to the darkness that there should be light.

Jesus has spoken into your life today. He declares you free from sin. He proclaims the year of the Lord's favor, release for those who are captured, and sight for those who have lost their vision. He speaks a new vocation for your days. He calls you to him, and he calls you to change the world. His words beckon you to draw near and empower you to move mountains. He asks you to speak with his voice, his authority, his commands, and his creativity. Be refreshed today. Put on the new nature given to you by Jesus, the creator of the world.

God, by your Word, create in me a clean heart, and renew a right spirit within me. Let me be refreshed in my soul today. Draw me close to you and help me to share this newness of life with those around me.

CONTENT

I know what it is to be in need, and I know what it is to have plenty. I have learned the secret of being content in any and every situation, whether well fed or hungry, whether living in plenty or in want.

PHILIPPIANS 4:12 NIV

We often think of contentment as the satisfaction of all our needs. If that were true, it would only be possible to be content when everything is perfect. God gives us the power and the peace to be okay even when everything around us is not.

Our decision-making and leadership is better when we learn to be content no matter the outcome. God frequently reminds us that true peace and contentment comes from our relationship with him and not the circumstances of our life.

God, please give me your perspective on my life. Help me to be content even when there are things I wish I could change. Keep me from acting in fear or worrying about things that are not how I wish they would be. Help me to trust that, no matter what, you are enough.

WITNESSES

We have all of these great witnesses who encircle us like clouds. So we must let go of every wound that has pierced us and the sin we so easily fall into. Then we will be able to run life's marathon race with passion and determination, for the path has been already marked out before us.

HEBREWS 12:1 TPT

We often perform better when someone is watching. We fight harder, strive further, and endure longer when we know others are paying attention. When we forget we're being watched, it becomes easier to succumb to our struggle. We might rest our defenses and end up tangled in things we wouldn't want others to see.

The everyday people in our lives surround us like a cloud. They are paying attention even when we might think they're not. Through them, God cheers for us to wrestle free from the things that would hinder our relationship with them and with him. Our hearts will fight for others more fiercely than we fight for ourselves.

Lord, I desire to be a good example for the people in my life. Please keep in my mind the truth that they are learning from my actions. Help me to trust that they are cheering for me, and that my successes are their successes. I believe they are worth any struggle, so please use them to inspire me to keep fighting.

GOD-BREATHED

All Scripture is God-breathed and is useful for teaching,
rebuking, correcting and training in righteousness,
so that the servant of God may be thoroughly equipped
for every good work.
2 TIMOTHY 3:16-17 NIV

There's a mysterious weight to the words of Scripture. It's easy to live with a more-or-less understanding of God's ideal life gleaned from the general idea of a verse. When we forgo the specific words of the Bible, we pull its punches a little bit.

Even though those around us might respond with glazed eyes, it is worth quoting relevant verses at relevant times. When we do, the life God has breathed into those words will help it come alive in the heart of the listener. The entire Bible is available to give just the right wisdom in just the right way.

God, I want to know your Word so I can apply it when opportunities arise. Help me to recall the verses I have read whenever they can be of use in my life or the lives of those around me. Encourage me to cling to your specific promises and not just my own paraphrases. Please sharpen my spiritual mind.

OBEDIENCE

"Go and gather together all the Jews of Susa and fast for me.
Do not eat or drink for three days, night or day. My maids and
I will do the same. And then, though it is against the law, I will
go in to see the king. If I must die, I must die."

ESTHER 4:16 NLT

God rarely asks us to produce a specific result. What he most frequently asks of us is simply obedience. We don't always know what the result might be, or even what God's will is in a certain moment. What we can be sure of is that he desires our devotion and commitment no matter the consequences.

Esther was unsure what would come of her action, but she was certain it was what she needed to do. The result would possibly be death, but her only concern was obedience. We can miss opportunities to serve God when we focus on the outcome. God's desire is to grow us through an experience and to have us trust him with whatever happens. Life with God is not about results; it is about obedience.

God, thank you for inviting me to be a part of what you are doing in the world. I confess I often worry about what might happen, instead of trusting you to work through every situation. Remind me that it pleases you when I obey, and that you want to take care of the rest.

DOING GOOD

As for you, brothers,
do not grow weary in doing good.
2 THESSALONIANS 3:13 ESV

It is worth it to keep doing what is right and good. It may be thankless and difficult, but it is always worth it. You might feel like it doesn't matter or that nobody notices how hard you work to live how God says to live. Perhaps you feel cheated because, despite your efforts, things just aren't working.

Keep going. Don't grow weary now. It's possible you won't see the results of your devotion, but nothing you give to God is fruitless. Lower your shoulder and keep pressing on. Every decision you make to do what is good gives God one more tool in his toolbox, and he is working to build something beautiful in your life. Keep going. It is worth it.

God, strengthen me to keep living how you ask me to live. Give me the endurance to make the decisions that please you, even when I'm worn. I pray you will restore my energy and help me to keep moving forward toward the life you want me to have. Thank you for being with me and for helping me live a life of doing good.

ADDING WORDS

"Every word of God is flawless;
he is a shield to those who take refuge in him.
Do not add to his words,
or he will rebuke you and prove you a liar."
PROVERBS 30:5-6 NIV

When we believe the Bible is on our side, we must take great care in how we convey its truth. It is good to understand what the Bible says about any situation, and following what God says helps us keep our integrity.

However, we must be careful to not exaggerate what Scripture says just because we think we're right. Let Scripture speak for itself. It's not our job to make the listener agree. We can simply share what the Bible says and trust that God will water and grow his truth for his purposes. God delights in our righteousness, but he also yearns for the righteousness of others.

Lord, help me to speak only your truth when helping others to see your light. Please protect me from injecting my own opinions into the work you're trying to do. I want to gladly share your Word with others, and I trust that it speaks for itself. Thank you for helping me be an amplifier for your truth instead of my own.

POINTING

"You search the Scriptures because you think they give you eternal life. But the Scriptures point to me! Yet you refuse to come to me to receive this life."

JOHN 5:39-40 NLT

Approaching Jesus can be intimidating. We're often afraid of what he might say, or ask, or already know. This fear will drive us to keep doing the "safer" spiritual discipline of just reading the Bible. Secretly, we hope that rushed prayers and memorized verses won't disrupt our lives too much.

But Jesus wants to disrupt our lives. He wants to shake up our routine and replace the parts that are lacking with the vibrant life we crave in the depths of our soul. Scripture is good precisely because it begs us to intimately connect with our Savior. Don't shy away from the spiritual tug of Scripture, frightening as it may be. If you let it lead you to Jesus, you will find what are you are looking for in every verse.

God, I believe that you want to bring satisfying life to every part of who I am. I confess that I sometimes hesitate to come to you for fear of what you might say. Please remind me that you are not interested in shame or judgment and that your core desire is for me to experience the life you created me to live.

INFINITELY MORE

All glory to God, who is able, through his mighty power at work within us, to accomplish infinitely more than we might ask or think.

EPHESIANS 3:20 NLT

God delights in surprising us. Like a father building an incredible treehouse for his child or a husband unveiling a dream vacation to his wife, God takes joy in doing things for us that exceed our expectations. He wants us to stare at him in wonder and realize that he is so much more impressive than we give him credit for.

Often, our dreams aren't big enough. We'd settle for a response to prayer that helps us just get by. Our heavenly Father wants so much more than that! We convince ourselves we aren't worth his time, but he says, "I want your life to be abundant, and I'm going to do that through you." The power of God is most beautifully demonstrated in his ability to exceed our expectations by working through us.

God, you are so much better than I can imagine. I know that even my grandest request seems small compared to what you want to accomplish through me. Help me to remember that you are at work in my life to create something better than I could ever create on my own.

BIGGER

I pray that out of his glorious riches he may strengthen you with power through his Spirit in your inner being, so that Christ may dwell in your hearts through faith. And I pray that you, being rooted and established in love, may have power, together with all the Lord's holy people, to grasp how wide and long and high and deep is the love of Christ.
EPHESIANS 3:16-18 NIV

God is so big that only he can show us how big he is. Our understanding of God begins with that first aha moment where his power becomes reality to us. That first taste creates a hunger for more, and we strive to learn all we can about God. As our understanding of God grows, so does his stature and power in our mind.

But eventually we realize that God exceeds our ability to understand. For some, this stunts their growth, as they refuse to chase the Holy Spirit into the "unknown." For believers, however, the "unknown" is an invitation to experience God in a way we can't explain. God's power, working within us, pushes out the boundaries we've created around our creator. God is actively working to help you experience even deeper satisfaction in your relationship with him.

God, thank you that I can never understand in this life just how truly wonderful you are. Thank you that every day is a chance to be amazed by your character. I pray that you will let my heart and soul continue where my mind wants to stop, and that I would feel the deep connection you desire with me.

MERCY THROUGH MENTORSHIP

Fathers, do not make your children angry,
but raise them with the training and teaching of the Lord.
EPHESIANS 6:4 NCV

For most people, the first understanding of God is directly connected to how they experienced their earthly father. Fathers are models of the Lord whether they intend to be or not. A child with a strict father will usually first assume God is judgmental. A child with an absent father will often first perceive God as uncaring. Fathers shape the lens through which children first see their Savior.

Through Jesus, God set his example of mercy through mentorship. It's easy to express reactionary anger when we are upset, but the Holy Spirit works to direct that angry energy into opportunities for growth and learning. When we do that, we paint a more accurate picture of God for the people in our lives.

God, I want others to know you. Please help me to conduct myself in a way that makes you look good. I pray that I will choose opportunities for growth over angry outbursts. Help me to see the best way—your way—to respond to my frustrations.

NOTHING WITHOUT

"I am the vine, you are the branches.
Those who abide in me and I in them bear much fruit,
because apart from me you can do nothing."
JOHN 15:5 NRSV

Many times we treat God like a turbo boost for life. For the most part we do our own thing, work hard to achieve our goals, and muscle through each day. But sometimes, when things are really hard, we finally relent and pray that God would help us over some particularly difficult hurdle in life.

If the above verse were written with regard to how many of us live, it would say "apart from me you can do most things." Of course, Jesus knew what he was saying. His point was clear: we shouldn't save our reliance on him like some sort of power-up. We are designed for constant connection to Christ. We function best, and really only function at all, when we choose to connect with God at all times, not just in tough times.

God, thank you for being my source of strength every day. I pray that I will reflexively turn to you in every situation instead of leaning on you only when I feel I've exhausted all other options. Thank you for caring about even the things that seem small or insignificant. I know life is more enjoyable when you're in all of it.

WEARY

Even youths shall faint and be weary, and young men shall fall exhausted; but they who wait for the Lord shall renew their strength; they shall mount up with wings like eagles; they shall run and not be weary; they shall walk and not faint.
ISAIAH 40:30-31 ESV

Whenever you feel worn out, it should serve as a reminder to connect with God. When we try to do things with our own power, we often find ourselves drained before the task is accomplished. But when we trust that God is at work and we are simply assisting him, we find a deep supply of energy to keep doing his will.

The next time you're exhausted, pause and talk to God. He may encourage you to keep going, he may insist you stop worrying and rest, or he may convict you to shed the added weight of a sin in your life. No matter how he responds, he promises to help you keep going in a way you might have thought impossible before.

Lord, thank you for giving me strength and energy when I feel I'm running out. Help me to continue experiencing your goodness even when I'm weary. I pray that I will realize the difference it makes to trust in you each day and that I will experience the vitality of living for you.

COMFORT

Even though I walk through the darkest valley,
I fear no evil;
for you are with me;
your rod and your staff—
they comfort me.
PSALM 23:4 NRSV

President Theodore Roosevelt famously said, "Speak softly and carry a big stick." Sometimes we focus too much on the gentle and comforting shepherd image of God, forgetting that one of the primary jobs of a shepherd is defender, which he is prepared to do.

It is in the darkest and most terrifying places that we are keenly aware of any source of safety. As our fight-or-flight reaction kicks in, we pay attention to anything that offers protection. Perhaps this is the reason that God sometimes leads us through dark periods of life, so we are reminded of the safety found in him. Your heavenly Father has every intention of protecting you with his might, and that fact should bring you deep peace when you're scared.

God, thank you for protecting me. I can take great comfort in knowing you are with me and you are powerful. Thank you for leading me through things that are intimidating, and for promising to help me fight when the time comes.

WORSHIP THE SPLENDOR

Honor the LORD for the glory of his name.
Worship the LORD in the splendor of his holiness.
The voice of the LORD echoes above the sea.
The God of glory thunders.
The LORD thunders over the mighty sea.
The voice of the LORD is powerful;
the voice of the LORD is majestic.
PSALM 29:2-4 NLT

Worshiping God is the only natural response to his power. When we find ourselves in seasons where worship is difficult, we can think it's because we don't feel close to him. Intimacy is often the result of worship, and worship is the result of focusing on God's power and goodness.

God's might is the source of the good things we experience in him. In times of difficulty we rely on his strength to protect us. In times of joy we celebrate his power working within us. In all situations we benefit from placing our focus on the splendor of God. In doing so, we pave the way for a deeper sense of intimacy with and connection to our Creator.

God, you are powerful and mighty. Help me to focus on your characteristics so that I can see my own life with a better perspective. I want to worship you no matter my circumstances. Your power is the most helpful thing for me each day.

IMITATE

I appeal to you, then,
be imitators of me.
1 CORINTHIANS 4:16 NRSV

You're a Christian not just because someone told you about Jesus, but because they also demonstrated what it means to live a Christ-centered life. The person who showed you is also following the example set for them by another, who is in turn copying yet another. For every Christian, there is an unbroken line of imitators that can be traced back to Jesus himself.

Your job, then, is to live in such a way that the chain continues. Is an invitation to live like you also an invitation to live like Jesus? Your imitation becomes an invitation, to those around you, into a satisfying life.

Lord, help me to live how you taught us to live. I want my life to be an example of what it means to follow you. I pray you will give me the strength to be an example to my friends and family of what it means to have a life devoted to you.

FULLNESS

To know the love of Christ that surpasses knowledge,
so that you may be filled with all the fullness of God.
EPHESIANS 3:19 NRSV

Christ's love brings fullness of life. It was his love for humanity that pushed him to sacrifice so much on our behalf. It is through that same love that we are invited into a rich and satisfying life. It is Christ's love that is the missing puzzle piece for all those who have yet to follow him.

The promise of Christ's love is that we have been made complete. Our own lives are transformed, and we are able to live with more power and purpose than we ever could alone. Through that power we can help others experience the same amazing love and invite them into the full life God intends for us.

God, please continue pouring into me. Help me to experience your love in a way that fills my life.

YOUNG EXAMPLES

Let no one despise you for your youth,
but set the believers an example in speech,
in conduct, in love, in faith, in purity.
1 TIMOTHY 4:12 ESV

It's our job to teach younger believers, and daily we should be looking for ways to explain or model something we wish for them to learn. Perhaps we feel like a spigot of knowledge, pouring out what we know into the young vessels. There is deep satisfaction in seeing what we've taught take hold in the lives of others.

We can easily view it as a one-way street, but while God is using us to teach others, he is also revealing himself to us through them. Some traits of the Lord are best demonstrated through youthful innocence and purity. If we pay close attention, we'll see the nature of God in younger Christians. When you do, celebrate it and encourage them. Let them know that God is using them right now, in their youth, to teach others about himself.

God, please give me eyes to see what younger believers can teach me about you. Help me to experience what they know about you, that I have yet to learn. And Lord, please remind me to thank them each time they remind me of who you are.

CALLED UP

"You should also look for able men among all the people, men who fear God, are trustworthy, and hate dishonest gain; set such men over them as officers over thousands, hundreds, fifties, and tens."

EXODUS 18:21 NRSV

When God is at work, he recruits men with hearts pointed toward him. He is less concerned about skill and experience, and more concerned with motivation and love. Men who are intentionally living for Jesus are the most likely to be called into faithful action.

It is in day-to-day life that people demonstrate their readiness for leadership. A man who waits for his marching orders to begin conditioning will find himself woefully underprepared. Instead, the most useful followers of Jesus are those who put his teachings into practice each day. It is never fruitless to follow Jesus with daily devotion.

God, I want to be the kind of man you can call on when you are at work around me. I also want to be the kind of man that others would seek out in their times of need. Please use my everyday experiences to strengthen and grow me into someone who can serve you well.

SAFETY IN NUMBERS

Where there is no guidance, a people falls,
but in an abundance of counselors there is safety.
PROVERBS 11:14 ESV

There is truth to the old saying, "It takes a village to raise a child." Parents can easily fall into the trap of believing that they alone must provide protection and instruction for their children. But living this way robs kids of experiencing the richness of many voices.

We are called to be both discerning and generous with the guidance of children. We should recognize the children that God has placed in our lives and be a part of their village! Then we set an example for Christian community and help their parents to provide a buffet of positive influence for their children. We are called to be a blessing to both our friends and their children.

God, thank you for the opportunity to be a positive voice who speaks into the life of children. I pray you will bless the families that I can influence by my words and actions. Through your Spirit, please use me to back up the things you are teaching through their parents.

WARNING AND PATIENCE

We urge you, brothers and sisters, warn those who are idle and disruptive, encourage the disheartened, help the weak, be patient with everyone.

1 THESSALONIANS 5:14 NIV

Correction and patience must go hand in hand. Correction without patience is anger. Patience without correction is avoidance. Being a godly leader requires both in equal balance.

The Bible urges us to follow God's example when encouraging right living in others. We are to point out God's expectations and highlight clearly when they're not met. This provides a chance to do the right thing. But the entire process falls apart if not done with encouragement, strength, and patience. Those are the three main ingredients of godly direction.

God, when times arise that I need to encourage others to live how you say to live, please help me correct them the way you say to correct. Give me the strength and patience to truly encourage change in their lives and continue to change me in the process as well.

TELL THEM

Parents will tell their children what you have done.
They will retell your mighty acts.
PSALM 145:4 NCV

We know an experience has profoundly changed us when we begin telling others about it. There is great power in stories, and the most powerful stories are those of God changing us. Throughout your life, God has worked to bring transformation, blessing, and wisdom. You're an expert in how God has worked in your life.

No doubt each of us has a favorite story. We connect to stories in an incredible way, and the fastest route to a person's heart is through story. You're an expert in your story and sharing the ways God has worked in your life is not only your responsibility but also one of the most effective ways to explain how God works within us. It helps the more famous stories of the Bible feel more alive when you know the same God is at work right now with someone you love. Tell people what the Lord has done, and is doing, in your life.

God, please help me to be authentic in talking with others about how you are at work. I want them to know you by hearing about the work you are doing in me. Remind me that my story is powerful and that you have given me experiences precisely so I can share them with others.

EVERYTHING YOU DO

Encourage the young men to live wisely. And you yourself must be an example to them by doing good works of every kind. Let everything you do reflect the integrity and seriousness of your teaching.

TITUS 2:6-7 NLT

The only way to demonstrate that we really mean what we say is to live it. Our actions are our primary way of teaching; our own lives are the ultimate visual aid for any life lesson we try to convey. If we want people to listen to our advice, we must live it clearly for them to see.

But if we want them to listen to our advice, we must also speak it. The best way to instruct is the one-two punch of teaching and modeling. We must live correctly and then explain why we have chosen to live that way. People around you will learn from your life, no matter what it teaches.

God, please help me to be consistent in what I teach to the people in my life. Give me the strength and wisdom for my life to serve as a wonderful lesson for what it means to be a man of God.

REST

It is useless for you to work so hard from early morning until late at night, anxiously working for food to eat; for God gives rest to his loved ones.
PSALM 127:2 NLT

Failure to rest is usually the result of failure to trust God. There are many valid things we could do with any hour of the day, and danger comes when we forget that rest is one of them. We were created to rest; in fact, the first full day that Creator and man spent together was a day of rest.

We know God disapproves of laziness, but we often forget that it is also sinful to never rest. No amount of work will ever supply the deep sleep and rest that God offers. He beckons us to rest so we can remember our dependence on him. When we do, we are more likely to depend on him on the busy days as well. Take time today to rest.

Lord, I know I need rest. Give me the courage to make time for rest by delaying or declining the things I need to do. Please provide peace that everything will be okay if I take time and obey your command to rest. I pray it will help me to trust even more that you are with me.

KNOW YOUR FLOCK

*Be sure you know the condition of your flocks,
give careful attention to your herds.*
PROVERBS 27:23 NIV

It's not enough to simply watch for trouble in the lives of our friends and family. We are called to keep our finger on the pulse of their heart and soul. We can easily lose that pulse in the normal rhythm of our everyday relationships, but as men we must give special care to our flock: the people in our care.

The beauty is that when trouble comes, we're more prepared for it. In fact, we're likely to catch it earlier if we already know the condition of another person's spiritual life. We're called to diligently keep watch over the ups and downs in the lives of the people we care most about.

God, please give me the ability to sense how my friends and family are doing spiritually. Help me remain consistent in my attention to their lives, and please highlight the things you want me to see.

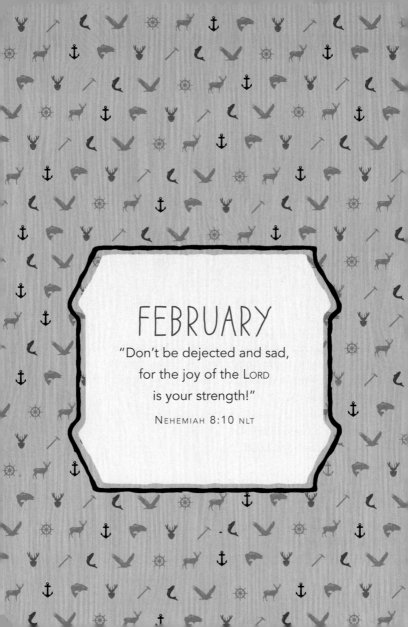

FEBRUARY

"Don't be dejected and sad,
for the joy of the LORD
is your strength!"

NEHEMIAH 8:10 NLT

ACT JUSTLY

He has shown you, O man, what is good;
and what does the LORD require of you.
but to do justly, to love mercy,
and to walk humbly with your God?

MICAH 6:8 NKJV

God has shown us what is good. Not merely through his law, although his law is good. Not only by dealing with those who reject those laws. Not only by keeping his Word. God shows us what is good through his Son, Jesus. Jesus was the physical representation of justice. He brought healing. He cast out demons. He brought hope. He righted wrongs. And, finally, he paid the penalty for our sin in an ultimate act of justice.

We act justly when we behave as he did. We can bring healing, cast out demons, bring hope, and right the wrongs around us, first in our homes and then in our churches, communities, and the world. To act justly is to remember that we love others because Jesus first loved us. God's justice is not only final; it is also ultimately complete. And it is utterly hopeful and hope filled. As we act justly with those around us, may it also be hope filled.

Lord, you've shown me what is good, in your Word and in your actions. History is filled with freedom and salvation. It's also filled with bondage and seemingly hopeless situations. Teach me to act justly in a world that so desperately needs it.

MERCY

The faithful love of the LORD never ends!
His mercies never cease.
Great is his faithfulness;
his mercies being afresh each morning.
LAMENTATIONS 3:22-23 NLT

"Mercy!" Perhaps you cried that out as an older brother or uncle twisted your arm behind your back or applied just the right amount of pressure in the wrong spot. "Mercy" is what we say when we give up, when we need deliverance from someone or something. Mercy is also what we need from a just God because of our disobedience to him. And mercy is what God offers to us. He gives this to us because without it, we are a poor and pitiable people. We are hopeless, lost.

Just as we loved it when that uncle would release us from his grip, we love it when we receive mercy from God, when we know we're caught in a twisted mess of life. But to "love mercy" here is not to love mercy received but mercy given. This is good. This is required: to love the giving of mercy to those who do not deserve it, just as we recognize the undeserved mercy from God. This week, consider mercy when what is deserved is punishment. This, after all, is God's heart.

God, I love receiving your mercy because I know just how much I need it. Help me to give that same mercy to those in need.

WALKING HUMBLY

*When pride comes, then comes disgrace,
but with the humble is wisdom.*
PROVERBS 11:2 ESV

I love to take walks, whether it be a leisurely stroll or a purposeful way of getting somewhere I need to be. To be honest, I prefer to go alone but I am intentional about inviting others to join me. Walking with people requires humility. Someone is going to want to walk faster or slower than the other. Someone will want to go look at something that the other may not want to see. Someone may want to walk farther. Or, they may want to just stop in the middle of the road and be done with it. In any of these situations, humility will be required of someone.

Walking with God is no different. His ways are not our ways. And he is the leader, the pacesetter. Where he goes, we follow. Our humility is in following him, step by step, walking with him. He leads with love. Walk humbly with God and bring others along, because we were not meant to take this journey alone.

God, I want to walk with you. I trust that you know where we are, where we are going, and when we will get there. Lead me with love.

SELF-SACRIFICE

"The Kingdom of Heaven is like a treasure that a man discovered hidden in a field. In his excitement, he hid it again and sold everything he owned to get enough money to buy the field."

MATTHEW 13:44 NLT

We sacrifice the most for the things we most desire. We will commit to a thirty-year loan to own a home and to up to a six-year loan for an automobile. We work forty, fifty, even sixty hours a week (or more) to get a promotion at work. And with each of these things comes a cost.

There is, however, something greater than any of the above. God's kingdom. Jesus tells us that God's kingdom is so valuable that it would be like finding a treasure hidden in a field, then selling everything we own to buy that field to get the treasure. What might it look like for us to pursue God's kingdom with such intensity? What might we have to give up for that to be the most important thing?

God, I have experienced the glory of your kingdom, and I want it to be my life's greatest pursuit. Please help me honestly evaluate my sacrifice for you.

MOST IMPORTANT LESSON

"This is how God loved the world:
He gave his one and only son,
so that everyone who believes in him
will not perish but have eternal life."

JOHN 3:16 NLT

This text is likely the most recognizable text in the Bible, if not in the English language. You will see it in the end zone at most football games and just behind the catcher or on the baseline at a baseball game. It will be just behind the backboard at a basketball game and along the racetrack at an automobile race. It will be held high in a town parade by churches and individuals alike. Why?

Because in it we find the most important lesson that there is: God loved us so much that he sent his Son, Jesus, to perish in our place. This is the gospel message in one simple sentence. Of all the things that we learn in life, it is this message that is the most important. A great way to remember the impact of this scripture is to read the verse, replacing "the world" and "everyone" with first our names and then the names of those around us. Do this often, and we will all know the greatest lesson.

Father, you loved us so much that sent your Son to pay for our sins. He took our place, perishing for us so we may have eternal life. You did this for each of us personally. Teach me to be grateful for it and to pass it on.

IDENTITY

You are no longer a slave but a child,
and if a child then also an heir, through God.
GALATIANS 4:7 NRSV

This is no small change of identity. From slave to son is a huge change. We are given the right status to walk hand in hand with our heavenly Father. We don't follow him around out of obligation but instead walk side by side with him as he calls us son.

The relationship we are given with God through Christ is an amazing opportunity to sit knee to knee with God and converse, to hug and to see the smile that only a father can give a child. A smile that says, "That man there is my son, and I love and am proud of him."

Thank you, God, for calling me son. Thank you that you smile upon me and call me your own. When I am discouraged, remind me that I am your child and have all that you have for me.

DON'T SHRINK

"I never shrank back from telling you what you needed to hear, either publicly or in your homes."
ACTS 20:20 NLT

As Paul was preparing to leave the elders from Ephesus, he essentially gave them his resignation notice. He told them that he loved them and that from day one it was his desire that they know Jesus and his good news. He spoke of his hard work among them, and how this often required confronting them with truth. Confronting others is one of the most difficult things that we do. When the person we will confront is a family member, it is even more difficult. But confrontation is a part of being a man. It is necessary.

When it came to telling people what they needed to hear, Paul did not shrink back, and as men, we must not be afraid to be honest with people and speak truth into their lives. What they need to hear beyond any other message is the truth of the gospel and the good news of Jesus Christ. We have to confront them on their sin and point them to Jesus as the one who took care of it. We must not shrink back.

I am thankful for the people in my life who did not shrink back from telling me a truth that I needed to hear. They demonstrated courage in doing so. Please give me that same courage to not shrink back from telling others what they need to hear.

HONORING PARENTS

Children, obey your parents because you belong to the Lord, for this is the right thing to do. "Honor your father and mother." This is the first commandment with a promise: If you honor your father and mother, "things will go well for you, and you will have a long life on the earth."

EPHESIANS 6:1-3 NLT

As children, we were under the authority of our parents and had to obey them. But in that obedience, we may or may not have honored them; this was determined by our attitude. As adults, while we are no longer bound to obey our parents, we are to honor them.

Think of what this demonstrates to those around us:

- We honor our parents when we ask for advice; this demonstrates that we view our parents as wise.
- We honor our parents when we speak kindly of them; this demonstrates respect.
- We honor our parents when we spend time with them; this demonstrates value.
- We honor our parents when we defer to an activity they would prefer; this demonstrates humility.

In each of these, we are showing others how we honor our parents, and they are learning by our example.

Lord, my parents have taught me so much about life. While imperfect, they sought to love me and care for me. Help me to honor their efforts by respecting and valuing them in ways that others see, so they will be blessed.

HOPE

The same thing is true of the words I speak.
They will not return to me empty.
They make the things happen that I want to happen,
and they succeed in doing what I send them to do.
ISAIAH 55:11 NCV

As godly men, we look for ways to teach and train others in the faith. We offer to take them to church, join our small group, or something as simple as sharing a meal so they can talk about their struggles and doubts. We pray for and with them. Even so, they sometimes make decisions that lead them away from Jesus. We are crushed, heartbroken, and frustrated. Does this sound familiar?

And yet, Isaiah 55:11 is so filled with hope. This Scripture teaches us that the faithfulness of God's Word is ever fruitful. His words are not pie-in-the-sky naiveté but truth. Promises. Believable. Inspired. Inspiring. Trustworthy. Full and complete. And they do everything that God sends them to do.

Father, I so much want people to know who you are. I want them to know and experience your power and majesty. I want them to know your peace and promises. I want them to come to you with their burdens and lay them at your feet and find rest. I want them to know that the joy of your salvation is greater than anything that might bring them temporary happiness here on earth. I want them to know you deeply and intimately. I want them to escape the sorrows of their sin and instead know freedom. I want each of these things and more, because you want them. I praise and thank you for your words of hope.

COURAGE

Be watchful, stand firm in the faith, act like men, be strong.
Let all that you do be done in love.
1 CORINTHIANS 16:13-14 ESV

There is a crisis of fatherhood today. The US Census Bureau says 24 million children (one in three) live in homes without their own dad. But children with dads involved in their life are more successful, more confident, more sociable, and less likely to have a list of adolescent problems. Clearly, dads play a large role in the success of children. These truths not only apply to biological fathers, but men who are willing to be spiritual fathers as well.

This verse includes four descriptions of a godly man. He is alert, stands firm in the faith, is strong in his courage, and loving. A challenging list! This describes a man who is engaged and aware of what's going on in people's lives. This is a man who is careful to pass along his faith by his words and also in the way he models it to those around him. This is a man with a purpose who doesn't give up when tests and conflicts arise. All of this is embodied in a bold love that makes him willing to put others first and treat them with respect. It takes courage to be a godly man, and even more so to be a godly "father". What younger men has God placed in your life who are in desperate need of a spiritual father?

God, being a spiritual father is an amazing privilege. With your help, I'm up for the challenge because people need me. Help me to be a man that makes a difference.

ENCOURAGE

*Fathers, do not provoke your children,
lest they become discouraged.*
COLOSSIANS 3:21 NKJV

The truth of this verse extends far beyond the relationship that a father has with his son. As men of God, we should not provoke anyone, but what did Paul mean by "provoke"? Earlier in this chapter, Paul told the Colossians to "put off" the things that lead to spiritual death: anger, wrath, malice, blasphemy, and lying. Each of these behaviors are provoking in nature. When we respond in these ways to the people in our lives, we are bound to discourage them.

Once we have taken off the things that lead to discouragement and death, we are to replace them. We do this when we "put on" the following: tender mercies, kindness, humility, meekness, longsuffering, bearing with one another, forgiveness of one another, and love. We are to be ruled by the peace of God, let Christ's words live within us, sing spiritual songs to one another, and do everything in the name of Jesus. When we do not provoke others, we encourage them to come to us and be in relationship with us. They will grow to trust us, and in turn they will demonstrate this new outfit to those around them. Be an encourager!

Father, help me evaluate the way I speak with the people around me. I want to be encouraging to them. Give me opportunities today to be humble, forgiving, peaceful, and kind.

EAT MEAT

You are like babies who need milk and cannot eat solid food.
For someone who lives on milk is still an infant and doesn't
know how to do what is right. Solid food is for those who are
mature, who through training who have the skill to recognize
the difference between right and wrong.
HEBREWS 5:12-14 NLT

There's nothing like a properly cooked piece of meat. After we have eaten it, we feel full and satisfied. As we grow and get older, our eating habits change and we adjust. What made us feel full at one year old barely makes a dent in our hunger when we are seven. And when we are seventeen? Forget it. Keeping up with that appetite is nearly impossible!

The same is true with spiritual nourishment. When we were young, we received spiritual milk; we were introduced to people like Adam and Eve, Noah, Moses, Samson, King David, Jesus, Mary, and perhaps the disciples, as well as basic Bible stories. But as we got older, we started digging into "meatier" concepts like sin, salvation, and the Trinity. We needed to learn the difference between right and wrong, true and false. What have you been feeding yourself lately? Are you still drinking from a bottle, or do you have your steak knife ready?

God, help me see how "hungry" I am, and to see that what I need is more of you. Let me be unsatisfied with a little bit of spiritual food and allow me to feast on the meat of your Word and be completely filled.

THE CLOSEST FISH

Then he said to them, "Follow me,
and I will make you fishers of men."
MATTHEW 4:19 NKJV

A lot of work goes into catching fish. We need to have all the right equipment: a rod and a reel, fishing line, bait and tackle, and a fishing license. If you don't want to fish from a dock or the shore, you'll need a boat. Then after accumulating all this gear, you'll be faced with the toughest decisions of all: where to fish and when to go. Often, we make these decisions by talking with family and friends or by going online. Because who wants to go fishing and catch nothing?

When Jesus spoke to his earliest disciples, he invited them to go "fishing" with him. But rather than go away to a far of place, Jesus and the disciples "fished for men" throughout the region of Galilee. Why? Because those "fish" were close by. At the end of his ministry, Jesus told his followers to go out and make disciples, beginning nearby in Jerusalem and then spreading to the ends of the earth. We, too, have fish near us. They are the people we interact with every day. We have all the equipment necessary, and because we have a relationship with these people, we know who to fish for and how to catch them. We are connected to them, knowing their eating habits, when they rest, and when they are active. Go fishing for them. Today.

God, I can be a fisher of men as well. Help me to see that you have given me all I need to catch them for you.

DISCIPLINE WITH LOVE

"The Lord disciplines those he loves,
and he punishes each one he accepts as his child."
HEBREWS 12:6 NLT

"This is going to hurt me more that it will hurt you." As a child you may have heard this phrase. Parents know the truth of this statement because, while discipline is part of being a parent, it is not a joyous one. Being corrected by a parent should not be vengeful punishment, but loving discipline. Loving discipline has one goal in mind: restoration. It seeks to bring people together, to right wrongs, to show that justice is possible, and to point to a time when all there will be is peace.

The greatest example of this is God's love for us. He disciplines us through the consequences of our actions and choices, and through the Scriptures and conviction from the Holy Spirit. He allows consequences because his desire is for us to be restored to him. This discipline reveals that we are not only loved by him, but that we belong to him. And this belonging came at great cost—the sacrifice of his Son for us. It truly did hurt him more than it hurt us.

Father, I am thankful for your discipline. It is designed to restore me to you and to make me more like your Son. As I experience your discipline, help me guard my heart and respond out of love.

DIVINE DISCIPLINE

As you endure this divine discipline, remember that God is treating you as his own children. Who ever heard of a child not disciplined by its father?

HEBREWS 12:7 NLT

"Who ever heard of a child not disciplined by its father?" The question asked in this verse is rhetorical, regardless of the answer. On one hand, our response is, "Of course I've not heard of this. Discipline of children is part of the parental responsibility." On the other, we say, "Yep, I knew kids like that growing up. They ran wild and caused all sorts of problems. And we have some kids on our street whose parents never confront their behavior."

When God disciplines us, he is showing to everyone that we are his. The fact that we endure it is the evidence that we are in the hands of a loving father. By default, a father must discipline his child. If not disciplined, the child seemingly belongs to no one.

God, you set the example for discipline. You allow me to endure it first because I need it, and second because it shows that you are indeed a loving father. If you let me run wild, it would say much about your character as well as mine. Help me to recognize that you discipline me because I belong to you.

STAY ALERT

Be sober, be vigilant; because your adversary the devil walks about like a roaring lion, seeking whom he may devour.
1 PETER 5:8 NKJV

The word sober in this verse has nothing to do with alcohol or drunkenness; here it means to have a clear mind, to be alert. To be vigilant means to be looking both outward and inward for something, to be ready. But ready for what?

The adversary. Our enemy, the devil. Sometimes we believe that this adversary is out sneaking around, hiding in the bushes or creeping in on us. But the imagery used here by the author of Hebrews is that of a roaring lion. We know he is coming. In fact, he is announcing himself. We hear him. The soberness and vigilance is not about looking for him to arrive, but about being prepared for his arrival. God works with us so we not only know the roar of this lion, but also know what to do when he arrives. He has shown us that we are best prepared when we are sober and vigilant.

Lord, my adversary is coming. I know he is because I can hear him. He is roaring and he wants to devour me. He wants to devour my friends and my family. Help me to be sober and clear minded. Help me to be vigilant and ready. And help me to teach others how to stand strong against him when he arrives.

JUST ONE GENERATION

When all that generation had been gathered to their fathers, another generation arose after them who did not know the LORD nor the work which He had done for Israel.

JUDGES 2:10 NKJV

A lot can happen in one generation. Nations can rise and nations can fall. Resources can be increased or lost forever. Just in one generation. Throughout Deuteronomy, we see God giving many instructions to Moses; they spoke about worship, the building of the tabernacle, and many other things. And in many instances, these instructions ended with God saying something like, "And when your children ask about why you do this, tell them that I delivered you out of slavery." The reason given was simple: to keep the people from forgetting what God had done. But in just one generation, the knowledge of the past was gone. The people still had the rituals to follow, but they didn't know why.

As men, it's our role to talk about the amazing things God does. We give glory and praise him for his deeds and work. We talk about the "why" because we need constant reminders of who God is. Let's keep talking about what God has done so the next generation remembers.

Father, it's so easy to forget. To forget what you have done, and to forget to pass our faith on to the next generation. We forget who you are, and we forget how you have delivered us from our sin. Help us to remember daily your love and sacrifice for us, and to share with others the hope and promise of delivery for them.

WASHING FEET

He got up from the table, took off his robe, wrapped a towel around his waist, and poured water into a basin. Then he began to wash the disciples' feet, drying them with the towel he had around him.

JOHN 13:4-5 NLT

Jesus was a servant and demonstrated this with his disciples the night before he died. After they entered the room where he would eat his final meal, he picked that moment to do the lowliest task a servant could do: wash feet. Jesus did this not out of false humility or to receive praise. In fact, one of his disciples, Peter, chastised him for it.

Men can wear a lot of hats: friend, co-worker, boss, son, brother, father, uncle, just to name a few. There are so many people in our lives we are called to serve and love. One of the easiest ways to share the gospel with them and to teach them the character of God is to serve them in the way Jesus served others. Each day, we have opportunities to wash the feet of those around us through selfless, and sometimes humiliating, acts of service. We can clean up their mess. We can show mercy and grace when judgment is warranted. We can consider them greater than ourselves and spend time with them in ways that honor them and not us. Serve like Jesus.

Master, I am the servant, you are my Lord. I am here to serve you so that others see you. Help me remember that when I serve the people in my life in honesty and humility, that I magnify you alone.

DISCERNMENT

"You must distinguish between the unclean and the clean."
LEVITICUS 11:47 NIV

Beginning in Genesis 3, we find humanity struggling to discern the difference between evil and good, and it is in this struggle that we find people making choices that separate them from God and other people. Cain failed to bring God a righteous offering. David didn't look away from Bathsheba. And while his son Solomon asked for (and received) wisdom from God, he was led astray. In the New Testament, we find Peter refusing to eat with Gentile believers.

We are no different. In Romans 12, we're told to be transformed by the renewing of our minds. These new minds teach us the difference between right and wrong, and then the Holy Spirit gives us the ability to choose right over the wrong. Finally, we pass this on to others. We do this when we tell people about God, life in Christ, and power from the Spirit, and when we encourage them to make right choices. As we pray for knowledge and wisdom, may we also ask for the desire to do the right thing.

God, your Word is clear about right and wrong. Through it, show and teach us what obedience looks like, and give me the courage to do what is good.

PHYSICAL TOUCH

The LORD said to Moses, "Take Joshua son of Nun, a man in whom is the spirit, and lay your hand on him. Give him some of your authority so the whole Israelite community will obey him."

NUMBERS 27:18, 20 NIV

Physical contact affirms what is being verbally communicated. We tell those we care about, "I love you" and often follow it with a hug, kiss, or pat on the back. When parents discipline their kids, they may place their hand on their shoulder to indicate their seriousness. Touch can provide a feeling of safety and security.

In Numbers, Moses is told by God to bring Joshua before the people and to lay his hand on Joshua, showing approval as power shifts from the aging Moses to the younger Joshua. In 1 Timothy 4, Paul tells a younger Timothy that Timothy received his gifts when the elders laid hands on him, and to live up to those gifts. As men, we must recognize the need for both verbal and physical communication. May we remember the power of loving, kind, appropriate, and frequent touch.

You are a God of touch. When you created man, you literally touched the dust of the earth to do so. You breathed life into our nostrils. When your Son, Jesus, was on earth, he healed many by physically touching them. And your Spirit literally dwells within us; we are your temple. Help me to value touch.

LONG-TERM PLANS

Salmon begot Boaz, and Boaz begot Obed;
Obed begot Jesse, and Jesse begot David.
RUTH 4:21-22 NKJV

What began as the story of a woman in search of someone to care for her daughter-in-law ended twenty-eight generations later with Jesus Christ. Boaz had no way of knowing this when he took Ruth as his wife. God, however, knew exactly what he was doing because he is interested in long-term plans.

Long-term plans are why, when he set up rules and regulations about worship, he told the parents to tell their children "why" when they asked questions about those rules and regulations. Long-term plans are why God considered the character of those whom he chose—and chooses—to lead his people. Long-term plans are why the same Gamliel who spoke up in defense of the apostles in Acts 5:33 was also the mentor of Saul, who was also called Paul (Acts 13:9). Long-term plans are the only reason why we even know the names of Ruth and Boaz. We have no idea what God will do with us, our children, our grandchildren, and beyond. But we participate in those plans when we are obedient today because we set each following generation on a trajectory of future obedience. Remember the long-term plans of God.

God, you are all-powerful, in every place, and all-knowing. You alone know what the future holds and the role that I and future generations will play. Help me to choose obedience to you today.

PREPARATION

Remember your Creator in the days of your youth.
ECCLESIASTES 12:1 NIV

Life is a journey, and it's a trip we only take once. Each of us on our own path. We cannot turn back time but can only move forward. With that irreversible permanence in mind, how important it is to be careful! And that is why the Bible instructs us to remember our Creator and seek first His Kingdom.

In all career paths, there is a requirement of training and preparation. If you want to be a lawyer, you must study the law. Future doctors study for many years to prepare for their career. Imagine a doctor saying, "I intend to practice medicine, but I have no desire to listen to what others have studied or researched about diseases and their remedies." No, certainly not. How foolish would we be to not listen to God's wisdom. The Bible is overflowing with stories of those that have gone ahead of us; and we have so much to learn and wisdom to glean from these passages. Take time to read and learn God's principles that are intended to prepare us for daily life.

Father, you have given us wisdom and truths to follow. Thank you for the gift of your words in our Bible. Create in me the desire to obey you in all things.

WELL DONE

"His master replied, 'Well done, good and faithful servant!
You have been faithful with a few things;
I will put you in charge of many things.
Come and share your master's happiness!'"
MATTHEW 25:23 NIV

There is only so much one can accomplish in a given day. There are actually twenty-three hours, fifty-six minutes, and four seconds in the average day. And in that time, a number of things need to be done:

- We will sleep.
- We will eat.
- We will go to work.
- We will praise God.
- We will spend time with family.

How can we do each of these things with the intent and purpose of glorifying God and being faithful to him? God has put us "in charge" of just a few things. The way to join in the happiness of God is to be faithful in the few things he has given us and take full advantage of every moment of each day. Then we will hear, "Well done."

God, there is both so little and so much time every day. Time passes by so quickly that at the end of the day, I sometimes wonder where it all went. Each day is a gift, and every moment an opportunity for faithfulness. Help me to serve you each day.

STAND STRONG

Keep yourselves in God's love as you wait for the mercy of our Lord Jesus Christ to bring you eternal life. Be merciful to those who doubt; save others by snatching them from the fire; to others show mercy mixed with fear—hating even the clothing stained by corrupt flesh.

JUDE 21-23 NIV

Waiting for things is not only an important part of life; doing so with patience is a trait of a believer in God. We are in the space between the resurrection and return of Christ, and as we wait, we show mercy, save others, and hate evil.

People are different, and each one will have a different temperament and personality. Perhaps you work with someone who is anxious and filled with doubts; be merciful, gracious, and kind—always. Maybe one of your friends is in grave danger; act decisively and quickly, for time is of the essence. Does a family member need to be convicted of sin? Share with that person the total character of God and talk about love and justice. God is merciful to us and has placed people in our lives that we might love them well. Know them and what they need.

Father, there are times when I doubt and am in need of mercy. Make me aware of your mercy that I may be merciful. Other times, the situation is pressing and I need an immediate evac! Help me see this in others. I know I have sins to be convicted of, so do that for me. Help me repent of my sin and point others to repent of theirs.

WHAT YOU WEAR

Since God chose you to be the holy people he loves, you must clothe yourselves with tenderhearted mercy, kindness, humility, gentleness, and patience.

COLOSSIANS 3:12 NLT

What kind of clothes should a man wear? A suit and tie for an important meeting? A uniform for work? Maybe a ratty T-shirt and jeans for oil changes and mowing? Or how about some casual Saturday clothes with his favorite team logo for the college football game?

The mixture of polyester and cotton isn't nearly as important as what a man wears in his heart and actions. For Christian men, this is especially true because, whether we like it or not, a follower of Christ is a strategic representative of God. What a Christian says and does has significant ramifications. So when we "put on" mercy in the midst of trouble, or when we choose patience over raising our voices in frustration or when we consistently encourage those around us, people will take notice. "If that's what God is like," they'll say, "then I can trust God."

God, help me to be clothed in your qualities and characteristics today. Let me be a proper representative for you to those around me.

DEVOTED TO PRAYER

Devote yourselves to prayer
with an alert mind and a thankful heart.
COLOSSIANS 4:2 NLT

Stop everything you're doing, even if just for a few minutes, and pray. Put aside your anxieties, put to rest your weighted burdens, and have a conversation with God. Take a moment to pray for your own relationship with God. What has he done in your life that makes you thankful? Where do you need to realign yourself with his Spirit? What requests, what needs, could you put in his hands? Take a moment to ask God what his plans are for you. Devote yourself to prayer.

Now take a moment to pray for the people in your life. What has God done in them that makes you thankful? Where do they need to realign their priorities with the Holy Spirit? What requests and what needs do they have that you could entrust to the Lord's hands? Take a moment to ask God what he sees when he looks upon them. Devote yourself to prayer.

God, remind me to be constantly talking with you. Don't let me neglect coming to you in prayer. May I become a devoted man of prayer for not only my own sake, but also for the sake of the people you have placed in my life.

EVERY OPPORTUNITY

Live wisely among those who are not believers,
and make the most of every opportunity.
Let your conversation be gracious and attractive
so that you will have the right response for everyone.
COLOSSIANS 4:5-6 NLT

Who are the people around you who need God? Take a deep breath, close your eyes, and consider those who are close to you that, for one reason or another, are not following God. Is there someone in your family? Perhaps one of your friends? A coworker? A neighbor? Having the right response for someone is not really about knowing how to win an argument. It's much more about living in such a way through the circumstances of life that others take notice. You want others to see a wellspring of strength and a daily resource in you. You want them to think, There's something different about him. He has a peace that I need.

When that moment comes, you'll want to be ready to share about the source of your strength and courage. It is in the everyday moments that your life has its greatest impact. How others see you in the routines, accidents, stresses, and relationships will reveal to them who you truly are and what you truly have. How you live in your everyday life could make the difference between someone finding God or continuing to live apart from him.

God, let me live consistently in your patterns every day, so I may be ready to share at any moment how great you are.

REPRESENTATIVE

We are Christ's ambassadors;
God is making his appeal through us.
We speak for Christ when we plead,
"Come back to God!"
2 CORINTHIANS 5:20 NLT

To "represent" someone means to "re-present" them. In other words, if you represent someone, it's as if you're making them present again. Make sense? No? Maybe? Okay, let's try to illustrate it this way:

Let's say there was a king who came to a land and did many good things for people. Let's say this king supplied daily bread, extended mercy to those in trouble, and gave himself on behalf of those in his kingdom. Then, let's say the king asked you to become his representative to those people. In effect, he was calling you to be his ambassador. He was entrusting you with his authority and words. When you would speak, the words you spoke would represent the king's words. When you would act, the patterns of your life would enact the king's grace or justice. As the king's representative, it would be as if the king was right there, living through you. And so it is with us as we live our lives for Christ, as his representatives.

God, let me speak as you would speak, act as you would act, and represent you to everyone I come in contact with today.

MARCH

"Don't be afraid,
for I am with you.
Don't be discouraged,
for I am your God.
I will strengthen you and help you.
I will hold you up
with my victorious right hand."

ISAIAH 41:10 NLT

STRONGER TOGETHER

Two are better than one, because they have a good return for their labor: If either of them falls down, one can help the other up. But pity anyone who falls and has no one to help them up.
ECCLESIASTES 4:9-10 NIV

Strength is so often defined as a man who needs no help. Our culture celebrates the stoic man who is able to face his battles singlehandedly. We see the lone wolf celebrated as the ultimate in masculine strength. Ironically, such a man is likely the weakest and most vulnerable type of man you'll find.

Only weak people believe that receiving help is a sign of weakness. In the same way that we delight in offering strength to others, there are others who are eager to offer their strength to us. We need only be courageous enough to seek help, and to keep seeking until we find it. When we do, we will find our strength multiplied by those we join with.

Lord, please keep me from believing the lie that I have to do things on my own. Help me to trust others to carry the weights of my life with me, just as I work to help others with their burdens. I pray that you will fill my life with people who help make me stronger.

IT'S WHAT'S INSIDE

The LORD said to Samuel, "Do not look on his appearance or on the height of his stature, because I have rejected him. For the LORD sees not as man sees: man looks on the outward appearance, but the LORD looks on the heart."

1 SAMUEL 16:7 ESV

God often chooses the unexpected man to accomplish his goals. This is because God's method of choosing tends to be much different, and much deeper, than how we tally the score. The only person we're likely to assess accurately is ourselves, and even then we often exchange God's criteria for one less fitting.

God is able to look at our hearts, and he often uncovers positive traits even we have overlooked. He draws out of us a deeper strength than we thought we possessed. He produces from us more than we thought ourselves capable of. God is actively working to draw the very best out of the core of who he made you to be.

God, help me to see myself and others the way you see us. Please grow in my heart the qualities you desire and keep me from focusing on traits that don't matter. Thank you for working to grow me.

COMPLETELY NEW

If anyone is in Christ, there is a new creation:
everything old has passed away;
see, everything has become new!
2 CORINTHIANS 5:17 NRSV

The promise of the Christian life is not a better life or an improved life. The promise of following Jesus is a completely new life! The transforming power of God is so strong that it actively erases our old desires and ways of thinking. It is when we forget this that we start to beat ourselves up. We carry the weight of our mistakes around, which slows our growth.

You are a new creation, having been made new simply by choosing to follow Jesus. You don't need to worry about your past any longer. Just keep living in the direction of Jesus.

God, thank you for making me new. I'm grateful that you did more than just polish me up or make me presentable; you completely re-created my way of living. Please help me to remember the powerful work you've done in me.

STRONGHOLD

The Lord is good, a stronghold in a day of trouble;
he protects those who take refuge in him.
NAHUM 1:7 NRSV

In order for God to protect us, we must run to him. God is good, and he promises to offer us safety in times of trouble. But the deal is we must go to him. We need to actively seek his help when trouble comes our way.

He does this so that we keep in mind the true source of strength. In the act of retreating to God, we make great advances against our enemy. In turning to the stronghold of God, we deal an incredible strike against everything meant to harm us. How can it harm us if it is what brings us closer to our Savior?

God, you are the true strength in my life. In times of weakness or danger, please call to me. I pray that I will hear your voice warning me to draw near to you. Thank you for using potentially harmful things as a way to bring me closer to you.

WORKING IN YOU

*God is working in you,
giving you the desire and the power
to do what pleases him.*
PHILIPPIANS 2:13 ESV

God does not give us a list of demands and leave us to sort it out. He uses his power to help strengthen us. He is both the motivation and the destination for our spiritual lives.

We can make the mistake of thinking we must please him in order to experience closeness with him when, in fact, the inverse is what happens. When we draw close to him, he begins to produce in us the desire to do what pleases him.

Lord, I confess I sometimes avoid you because I'm afraid I'm not living how you want me to live. I pray you will help me realize that you are the source of the daily strength I need to live for you. Help me to come to you so you can grow healthy desires in me.

PEACE AND STRENGTH

The LORD gives his people strength.
The LORD blesses them with peace.
PSALM 29:11 NLT

Both strength and peace are things we often think of as being from within. Inner strength and inner peace are common phrases. While it's true that we perhaps experience those things internally, the source of them is both external and eternal. God gives us strength and blesses us with peace.

When we go through challenging times, we can be tempted to "dig deep" inside ourselves to find the strength to carry on. The truth is we should "reach out" to the source of that strength. If we feel we have nothing left, it's a sign that we are looking in the wrong place for peace or perseverance. The wonderful news is there is an endless supply, and God wants to bless us with both strength and peace.

God, thank you for giving me strength to face difficult challenges. And thank you for going even further, and for offering peace even in incredibly hard times. You are the source of all I need, and I am grateful.

WISDOM

With God are wisdom and might;
he has counsel and understanding.
JOB 12:13 ESV

It's no accident that God is the supplier of everything we need in life, be it strength, peace, or wisdom. When the Creator set up the universe, he did it in a way that we would be naturally drawn to him at every turn.

God and wisdom are one and the same. As the Creator, God is innately correct, wise, and right. Because of this, when we are closely aligned with our heavenly Father, we are more likely to know which decisions we need to make. The act of decision-making becomes an act of worship as we rely on our relationship with God to lead the way.

God, I am glad your wisdom and understanding are so great. And I am thankful that you choose to use your power to help me live how you created me to live. Please guide me and help me to end up where you desire me to be.

GROWING GOOD

Let us not become weary in doing good,
for at the proper time we will reap a harvest
if we do not give up.
GALATIANS 6:9 NIV

Every time we make the decision to do good, we start a countdown until the inevitable moment when we ask, "Is it worth it?" If we're honest, there are plenty of days when it feels like doing good isn't everything it's cracked up to be. People don't notice, life is still hard, and sometimes it seems like more trouble than it's worth.

Don't give up. Each time you do good a seed is planted, and a life centered around Jesus causes those seeds to grow and grow. We usually don't know the result of every good deed, but we can trust that God does and that he is helping them grow to their fullest potential. The more seeds of good you plant in your life, the more likely it is for your life to become vibrant and full.

God, sometimes I grow tired of working to do what is right; it often feels like an unfair fight. Please help me to trust that you are working through me each time I choose to do what is right. Please bless me with a chance to see some of the fruit of following your way.

SPEAKING LIFE

"Don't be afraid," he said, "for you are very precious to God. Peace! Be encouraged! Be strong!" As he spoke these words to me, I suddenly felt stronger and said to him, "Please speak to me, my lord, for you have strengthened me."

DANIEL 10:19 NLT

God's words bring life. Whether they come through Scripture, through family or friends, or from some unexpected place, they have the power to invigorate us at our very core. When we actively search for what God is speaking to us, we will find a vitality we might otherwise miss.

We can also speak those words to others to bring them life. We may be hesitant to intrude with Scripture when speaking to our family or friends, but we should be courageous enough to speak life to them as well. God has gifted us with the wonderful power of his words, and he encourages us to share them freely.

God, thank you for speaking life into me. Your words have the power to heal, direct, and strengthen. Please help me to share timely wisdom from you in the lives of those around me.

CHOSEN

You are a chosen race, a royal priesthood, a holy nation, God's own people, in order that you may proclaim the mighty acts of him who called you out of darkness into his marvelous light. Once you were not a people, but now you are God's people; once you had not received mercy, but now you have received mercy.

1 PETER 2:9-10 NRSV

God intentionally picked you. He didn't settle for you, and he didn't begrudgingly accept you; he chose you on purpose and for a purpose. You have been called into a role of great significance: you're an ambassador for Jesus Christ himself.

You're invited to tell anyone who will listen of the great change God has brought in you. You're encouraged to explain that such transformation is available to them as well. You have an endless supply of spiritual VIP passes to hand out. Let others know how important they are to God.

Father, thank you for choosing me. Thank you for making me different. Thank you for accepting me instead of rejecting me. Please give me opportunities to tell others about the life you invite them to live.

HOPE

Hope deferred makes the heart sick,
but a dream fulfilled is a tree of life.
PROVERBS 13:12 NLT

Don't put off hope. It's far too easy for our worries to shush the dreaming voice that asks, "What if?" We then delay in pursuing our deepest desires under the guise of safety or prudence. God invites us into adventure, and we reply with, "Someday." Replacing hope with waiting leads to an unhealthy life.

True peace comes from seizing the invitation to live a God-centered life. It almost always requires risk, but the reward is the rich and satisfying life we were created to live. People will not be shaped by "someday," but they will be forever transformed by daring to ask, "What if?"

God, I want to chase the dreams you've instilled in me. Please help me to fulfill the purpose you have for me, and to experience you by not waiting for what I hope will someday happen. Thank you for desiring a life of fullness for me.

DEPENDENCE IN CHRIST

God chose what is foolish in the world to shame the wise;
God chose what is weak in the world to shame the strong.
1 CORINTHIANS 1:27 ESV

As a man, you'll need to showcase not strength but life-dependent weakness to the creator of the universe—God. People don't need a superman who can fix all the unsolvable problems of the world; they need a committed, God-structured man who lives his life on his knees in total submission to the Lord.

They need to see the air you breathe (John 3:5-6), the bread you eat (6:48), the God who leads your life (15:5), and the obedience that comes by faith (8:31; 14:21, 23). Be intentional about living dependently and relying on the strength of God. These ideas are not contrasting in the Lord, but complementary to faithful living.

Heavenly Father, I come to you through the blood of the cross. Teach me to live my life in total dependence. May your Spirit align me with your Word and may my heart's affection be stirred to your truth. Teach me to acknowledge my weaknesses so I can lean on your strength. Teach me to model dependence in you to the friends and family you've blessed me with. Thank you that you're my strength, my rock, and my shield. Carry me today for your name sake's.

OVERCOMING PROCRASTINATION

If a man is lazy, the rafters sag;
if his hands are idle, the house leaks.
ECCLESIASTES 10:18 NIV

It may seem harsh, but laziness is a learned behavior. You may clear your dishes as soon as you're done eating and put them right into the dishwasher. Or you may leave your dirty dishes lying around and only wash them once you are looking for a plate to use. One is a disciplined behavior, and one reeks of procrastination. Both are learned with much practice.

It took time to develop a disciplined approach to household chores. In the same way it takes time to develop patterns of procrastination. The good news is, if you've learned to be a fantastic procrastinator, you can also learn to be a wonderfully disciplined and proactive man.

Lord Jesus, I thank you for your cross. May your Spirit grant me the power to change my ways in which I've let procrastination become my norm.

TEACH WITH TRAJECTORY

Set your minds on things that are above,
not on things that are on earth.
COLOSSIANS 3:2 ESV

With the instantaneous lures of our modern day, we need to see the value of viewing life through the lens of trajectory. We need to understand the truth that the choices made today impact the pathways for tomorrow, and that life is not merely what our eyes can see, but what the Lord has promised (Psalm 119:154).

And yet, we don't just look toward the future, but set our minds on eternity. The love, compassion, sacrifice, and service forged in these days for the sake of the gospel will have a ripple effect for eternity (Matthew 25:29-30). Let us be the people of God who operate within the confines of life for the eternal glory of God.

Father God, I praise you for the salvation you grant to me through the Lord Jesus Christ. It is by his work that my eternal destiny has been forever changed. Help me to live my life with eternity in view. Remind me that my choices should be seasoned with a trajectory toward your eternal kingdom. Teach me to walk in such a way as to set my gaze upon the Lord Jesus Christ.

CHARACTER

I therefore, a prisoner for the Lord, urge you to walk in a manner worthy of the calling to which you have been called.
EPHESIANS 4:1 ESV

Walking with integrity and character is the hallmark of the Christian faith. Not that we can merit salvation. But the fruit of our salvation produces in us a coherence to the commandments of God (1 John 5:3). Our call to salvation, is not to an isolation away from God's decree, but rather to exemplify his character, quality, and virtue.

The father's decree, then, is to lead his children not toward individualism, but rather to be a unique image bearer that reflects the grandeur, wonder, and glory of God (Romans 8:29; Ephesians 4:23-24; Colossians 3:10). Model character in your daily living and teach Christian virtue through the life, death, burial, and resurrection of Jesus Christ.

Father God, may your Spirit empower me through the blood of Christ to walk in a manner that is worthy of your call, for you called me. May the virtue and character that I reflect be honoring to your name. Grant me the grace to confess when I fail and the compassion to extend when others do likewise. May my life be saturated by your grace and solidified by your goodness.

IDENTITY

Jesus said to them, "Truly, truly, I say to you, the Son can do nothing of his own accord, but only what he sees the Father doing. For whatever the Father does, that the Son does likewise."
JOHN 5:19 ESV

Jesus, eternally generated by the Father, found his identity in him. Sons will grasp their value and worth by the display of love, grace, and affection that is afforded to them by their earthly fathers. Yet our earthly fathers often fail us and fall short of this lofty ideal.

As we look to Christ, the founder and perfecter of our faith (Hebrews 12:2), let the river of life flow from him into you with constant currency. This will form and establish a foundation for a Christ-centered identity that is firmly grounded in biblical truth. Identity, then, is grounded in the Creator, not creation (Romans 1:23). Usher yourself to the foot of the cross that you may find your creative purpose in the one who grants purpose.

Lord Jesus, I thank you that your sacrificial love granted me access to be called a child of God. It is through my union with you that I am adopted into your family. Help me to find my value and worth in you. Help me to be a vessel through which others will experience the beauty and majesty of your great love. May they truly find themselves when they root themselves into your life-giving love. Grant it to us for your name's sake.

STOREHOUSE OF WEALTH

I have stored up your word in my heart,
that I might not sin against you.
PSALM 119:11 ESV

In an age of information, may the fountain of your lips be filled with the Word of God. May the truth of his Word flow from your mouth into the hearts of those around you. How gracious would God be to allow your daily usage of words to be filled with his life-giving truths. And how equally amazing would he be to have your friends and family be recipients of such treasures.

Be intentional about having the Scriptures be the centralizing principle in your life and model a seriousness in handling the text. Saturate the minds of your loved ones, remembering that Jesus said, "Apart from me you can do nothing" (John 15:5). Abide! Be a storehouse of beauty that exudes truth to all you encounter.

Jesus, incline my heart to your ways and etch in my mouth your words. Draw my affections that they would be thrilled at the beauty of your truth. Stir in me a great adoration for the Scriptures that overflows into the hearts and minds of the people in my life. Give them ready ears and fertile hearts to embrace the seeds of life. And guard our hearts from the evil one who seeks to kill and destroy. May your Spirit be ever present in pointing our eyes to you. I lift up these prayers for the glory of your name and the joy of your people.

GRATEFUL HEARTS

Children are a heritage from the LORD,
the fruit of the womb a reward.
PSALM 127:3 ESV

Many men treat their cars with extra care and precise precision. The reason is because they understand the value and worth of the vehicle that they pour their time into. The Scriptures tell us that children are a blessing from the Lord. They embody the miracle of life that only God can provide while resembling his beauty, majesty, and grandeur in being made in his image.

Take a moment to reflect upon the children that God has brought into your life; whether they are sons, nephews, neighbors, or the ones that always seem to scamper underfoot throughout the church foyer. Realize that God has granted you the opportunity to show these children that their lives have value, dignity, and worth. Shower the children in your life with the love that flows from the Father through Christ Jesus.

Father God, I praise you for your unending love and mercy. It is by your grace that I'm granted the privilege to be called a child of God. My value and worth are intrinsically rooted in who I am in you. Lord Jesus, teach me to see through your eyes, and help me to cherish children in a way that would bring you glory. Thank you, Lord Jesus.

RESPECT

Hear, my son, your father's instruction,
and forsake not your mother's teaching.
PROVERBS 1:8 ESV

Respect for authority is a trait learned by observing a father who lives it well. The value of community and the profit of parents is understood by the tutelage and guidance of a fatherly figure. No earthly father is perfect, but when submitted to God they will instill a posture of respect that will permeate into their entire family.

Take some time today to reflect upon the father that God gave to you. What instruction did he provide that you carry with you to this day?

Lord, remind me of the instruction that my father provided. Help me to overlook his shortcomings and view him as you want me to see him.

SUPREMACY OF CHRIST

Since therefore the children share in flesh and blood, he himself likewise partook of the same things, that through death he might destroy the one who has the power of death that is, the devil.
HEBREWS 2:14 ESV

Children have an innate ability to sense the inaccuracy of ordinary life. Not only can they detect the inconsistencies of their parents, but they also often find in themselves the disparity that is rooted in their fallenness. As we age, it is essential that we bring to the forefront the colossal shortcomings that surface, in order to magnify the supremacy of the cross.

The charge for men is not to sweep these blunders under the rug, but to recognize that the cross of Christ cleanses us from all discrepancies. Though the sinfulness of our hearts can be heinous and, at times, unbearable, the magnitude of the cross conveys the message that the love of Christ stretches as far as the east is from the west (Psalm 103:12). Point your life toward the cross of Christ and make your home at his feet.

Lord Jesus, forgive me for the times when I move away from the cross and assume that I have developed beyond its impact. Teach me to rest at the foot of your cross where salvation, restoration, and reconciliation is found. Teach me to model and teach those in my life to be saturated by the gospel. Grant us the grace to ground ourselves in your goodness, and to always be stirred by the glorious cross.

LOVE THE CHURCH

*By this we know that we love the children of God,
when we love God and obey his commandments.*
1 JOHN 5:2 ESV

Model a great affinity toward the community of saints. This is sustained not by the self-generated will, but by a proper perspective of the biblical scope inflamed by the Holy Spirit. Being infused into the local assembly of saints will grant you the capacity to see life in God's larger scale.

Service to the children of God will create a disposition that will align you with God's redemptive work in using the church to bring forth restoration through Jesus Christ. We all long to be a part of something that is greater than ourselves. It is through the church that the manifold wisdom of God might now be made known to the rulers and authorities in the heavenly places (Ephesians 3:10).

Jesus, grant me an affection for your people that I may faithfully serve them for your name. Teach me to pour out myself for the good of your people and the joy of my heart.

TRANSPARENCY

If we confess our sins,
he is faithful and just to forgive us our sins
and to cleanse us from all unrighteousness.
1 JOHN 1:9 ESV

Strength, from a biblical perspective, is not an innate or self-generated sustenance; rather, it is grounded in a deep dependency on the Lord (Psalm 18:2). Confession of sin acknowledges the inability of the self and gravitates toward the one true God that sustains, restores, and redeems.

As a man, it is imperative to demonstrate the humility of confession, first to the Lord and second to your friends and family, which will embody a transparency that evokes the fruit of the Spirit (Galatians 5:22-23). Not only does it demonstrate the supremacy of Christ in your life, but it also models a clear picture of gospel living.

Lord Jesus, help me to not lean on my own righteousness. Teach me a humility that will make much of you.

FOLLOW IN HIS FOOTSTEPS

Whoever says he abides in him
ought to walk in the same way in which he walked.
1 JOHN 2:6 ESV

As a young athlete, you may have watched the greatest basketball player in the world, Michael Jordan. After an intense and gripping game, you may have even found yourself at the local court, shooting fadeaways and attempting acrobatic lay-ups with your tongue hanging out.

Likewise, we are not to become our own man per se; we are to mimic and imitate the God-man himself. He has come to show us what true humanity looks like, and by his Spirit we are to emulate him. As you walk through today, ask the Spirit to align your heart with his ways for his glory.

Lord, grant me the favor to walk in your ways. Incline my heart and stir my affections to your truth.

RELATIONSHIPS

As iron sharpens iron,
so a friend sharpens a friend.
PROVERBS 27:17 NLT

This verse from Proverbs produces such strong mental imagery. One can almost see the blacksmith's hammer poised momentarily above his head before it descends with a resounding clang on the glinting broadside of a dull sword. Or perhaps the scene shifts to the midst of a heated battle where men's fates are sealed as swords collide. Whether you side more with the vision of the blacksmith or the soldier, there is a seemingly violent and almost destructive nature to this process of iron sharpening iron. What an interesting picture the author of this Proverb chose to represent friendship.

Do you have iron in your life? That person who either attacks or defends in any given situation. Or maybe they just constantly bang against you, flattening you more and more with each blow. While we may prefer to be with people who are easygoing and always agree with us, it is these seemingly more contentious relationships that sharpen our character. As we parry with them back and forth our arguments are honed and convictions solidified. If nothing else, they give us so many opportunities to practice patience, forgiveness, and grace. But let us not forget, that we give others those same opportunities as we are the iron in their lives as well.

God, help me to love the people you have placed in my life even if it's uncomfortable. I am willing to endure the hard work of developing my character, while helping others do the same.

HOLINESS

Strive for peace with everyone,
and for the holiness without which no one will see the Lord.
HEBREWS 12:14 ESV

Autonomous identity is what society etches into the minds and hearts of its people. Uniqueness is pursued in order to standout, be distinct, and find ourselves in a class of our own. Yet what the biblical data conveys is a wholeness that is contingent upon linking oneself to the creator God, which brings forth a sanctity that sets us apart.

Holiness, meaning to be set apart, is obtained through a divine union with him though the work and person of Jesus Christ. Our distinction from the world is our disposition, through the rebirth of Christ, to live counterculturally, and to embody the new nature that is grounded in the Spirit. Pursue holiness through the access of the Spirit for the glory and fame of his name.

Lord Jesus, thank you for your sacrificial love, which granted me salvation. Thank you for imputing in me a righteousness from the Lord. Transform my heart so that it will be sensitive to your truth.

GROW IN MATURITY

Flee youthful passions and pursue righteousness, faith,
love, and peace, along with those who call on the Lord
from a pure heart.
2 TIMOTHY 2:22 ESV

Biblical manhood is not saturated with shallow definitions of bench press markings, sexual mischievousness, or financial achievement. A godly man is defined by his Christlike attitude that is expressed in consistent sacrificial servitude for the good of others and the joy of their hearts.

Maturing men seek to grow in pouring themselves out for the development of their loved ones while continuously being poured into through the mercies of the gospel. Righteousness, genuine faith, selfless love, and gentle peace are characteristics that describe the mark of a godly man.

Lord, help me to grow into the man you have called me to be. Align my heart with your purposes. Grant me a steadfastness in your truth.

SUBMIT TO MENTORSHIP

Follow the pattern of the sound words that you have heard from me, in faith and love that are in Christ Jesus.
2 TIMOTHY 1:13 ESV

You can only lead as far as you are being led! The task of leadership is not for the faint of heart. To properly take hold of the biblical mandate to shine forth the character of Christ you must be undergirded by the guidance of a biblically saturated individual who engages the blind spots of life. It is no small feat or fancy cliché that the biblical imagery consists of iron sharpens iron, and one man sharpens another (Proverbs 27:17).

Find solid men to surround yourself with. Growth occurs by being with people who will challenge you. Scripture says, "Whoever walks with the wise becomes wise, but the companion of fools will suffer harm" (Proverbs 13:20).

Lord Jesus, bring into my life a mentor who will point me toward you. Help me to trust and open myself to his critique. Bring forth growth and development that will honor your name.

TRAINING FOR A MARATHON

Rather train yourself for godliness.
1 TIMOTHY 4:7 ESV

"Rome wasn't built in a day."

"Olympic athletes don't shatter world records on their first day."

"Ball games are won in the off season."

"Preparation allows you to play fast."

All these sayings are marks, within athletic or warlike scenarios, that paint a picture of process. Though we are sold on the motto "quicker is better," the spiritual development of the heart takes time to marinate. The character of a man takes time to ripen. Don't take shortcuts in your sanctity, and don't despise the process. Buckle yourself in for the long haul and embrace the fact that you are a work in progress.

Jesus, grant me the patience to endure my own personal development. Give me zeal to pursue your goodness. Help me to keep my eyes on you, that I might not measure myself against anything else.

SEARCH THE INTENTIONS

The aim of our charge is love that issues from a pure heart and a good conscience and a sincere faith.

1 TIMOTHY 1:5 ESV

Be sensitive to the motives of your heart and keep watch on the intentions of your deeds. Saturate yourselves with the person of Christ, that his love might manifest itself in sacrificial deeds that will be a fragrant offering and sacrifice to God (Ephesians 5:2).

Center your aim on the gospel, using the cross of Christ as the model to measure all your expressions of love.

Lord Jesus, search the depths of my heart and reveal the severity of my sin. Pull me toward the cross that I may look at your goodness. May the sweetness of your love be the standard of my actions.

THANKFULNESS

We ought always to give thanks to God for you, brothers beloved by the Lord, because God chose you as the first fruits to be saved, through sanctification by the Spirit and belief in the truth.

2 THESSALONIANS 2:13 ESV

Gratitude postures the heart to not terminate one's thoughts, ambitions, and goals, but to see the gifts that have been given, ultimately, by God. In turn, we'll live in a manner that brings him praise.

There is a tendency to be inwardly focused and, as a result, meditate upon all the things that we don't have. Thankfulness, on the contrary, centers its attention on the Blesser who has given to us beyond all comprehension. Eternal life. Bountiful meals. Amazing shelter. A beautiful family. Be thankful that in his providence you are blessed beyond comparison.

Lord Jesus, stir in me a heart of gratitude. Help me to be aware of your blessings in my life. Assist me in not forsaking your goodness but seeing your faithfulness throughout my life.

HOLINESS THROUGH GOD

God has not called us for impurity,
but in holiness.
1 THESSALONIANS 4:7 ESV

In an age of relativism, saturate your mind with a robust biblical view of the triune God of the universe. Do not settle for small glimpses of him but be filled in awe with the mighty pictures that Scripture paints of our Creator.

Meditate on the distinction between the creation and the Creator (Genesis 1:1). Marvel at the notions that he is everlasting, and we are merely a mist within the wind (James 4:14). Ground yourself with the idea that the confines of time are not able to restrain him. Only then can we have a proper respect for holiness and begin to pursue it through the work of the cross.

Jesus, grant me the desire to capture a clear understanding of you. May my thoughts of you be full of substance and richness.

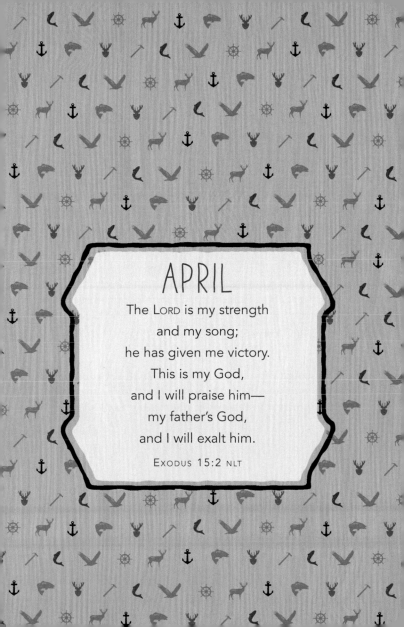

APRIL

The LORD is my strength
and my song;
he has given me victory.
This is my God,
and I will praise him—
my father's God,
and I will exalt him.

EXODUS 15:2 NLT

MARINATE IN THE WORD

Let the Word of Christ dwell in you richly,
teaching and admonishing one another in all wisdom,
singing psalms and hymns and spiritual songs,
with thankfulness in your hearts to God.
COLOSSIANS 3:16 ESV

We serve and lead out of the wealth (or lack thereof) that is stored up in our hearts. The value of life that permeates from our lives is intrinsically linked to the life that is within us. This life is not inherently ours; it's the breath of God that is blown into us through his Word.

Therefore, saturate yourself with his breath and continue to root yourself in the life source of God through the living Word. Only then can you begin to serve in such a way as to have the eternal impact that God has designed for you. This was his intended purpose for you as an image bearer of God.

Lord Jesus, grant me a hunger and thirst for your Word that my heart would be a fountain that stores your truth. May the words that flow from my mouth be filled with life.

UNITING LOVE

Above all these put on love,
which binds everything together in perfect harmony.
COLOSSIANS 3:14 ESV

As men, we tend to lean toward one of two extremes with ourselves: over-discipline or under-discipline. Some of us have a natural tendency toward being overdisciplined because we strive for perfection. Therefore, we seek to maintain order often at the expense of being harsh with ourselves and those around us (Ephesians 6:2). Others prefer an underdisciplined lifestyle because they fall prey to laziness or don't want to deal with the responsibilities of life.

However, the biblical perspective brings balance that is produced by a sacrificial love, grounded in biblical commandments. Embody a Christlikeness that expresses itself in grace and truth (John 1:14).

Lord, may your Spirit bring forth unity that expresses itself in love. May the impulse of my heart be to personify your compassion, mercy, and grace.

ANXIETY STEALS

Do not be anxious about anything, but in everything by prayer and supplication with thanksgiving let your request be made known to God.
PHILIPPIANS 4:6 ESV

Today, the pressures of getting there (wherever there is) is the undergirding drive and influence that stimulates a posture of anxiety that steals the beauty of the now. What will best serve your own heart is the ability to strive toward God's purpose while simultaneously embracing your current season of life. Don't look ahead at the price of neglecting what the Lord has blessed you with now.

Whether you are in a season of sorrow or joy, plenty or want, chaos or peace, make the best use of the time (Ephesians 5:16) and live each day with a zeal for the Lord. Give thanks to the Lord for blessing you in your current season of life, and don't waste these learning opportunities by looking ahead to a season of life that you haven't even reached yet.

Lord Jesus, forgive me for not trusting you. Posture my heart in a fashion of hope that grounds itself in who you are. Grant me a proper view of you.

CHRIST-CENTERED AIM

I press on toward the goal for the prize of the upward call of God in Christ Jesus.
PHILIPPIANS 3:14 ESV

In the daily grind of life, it's imperative to see and understand the undergirding principles that drive the things we seek to do and accomplish. It's not enough to merely mule through the motions; we need to continuously evaluate the motives and intentions of our heart in order to clearly see the motivating factors that fuel our life.

Without such evaluation, we will begin to place a weight upon our family, friends, or career that they are not meant to carry. We will ask our loved ones to fulfill in us what only Christ Jesus was meant to fill. Therefore, we must fight valiantly to preach the gospel into our heart and keep center the person and work of Jesus Christ. Without such admonition, we are bound to crush the very people we love.

Jesus, search the depths of my heart and incline my mind to your ways. May I meditate upon your precepts and find joy in your commands.

DISRUPTIVE PERVERSION

Sexual immorality and all impurity or covetousness must not even be named among you, as is proper among saints.
EPHESIANS 5:3 ESV

The institution of marriage is meant to display the beauty and mystery of God's redeeming work in reconciling the church to himself (Ephesians 5:32). The nucleus of the family is a shadow of God's eternal inheritance fulfilled in the person of Christ (Ephesians 1:14). All these images are to be compounded in the kingdom of God.

Sexual immorality is the attempt of the evil one to destroy, thwart, and diminish God's redemptive picture (Romans 1:24-25). The health and vitality of your family, present or future, points far beyond your own personal achievements, navigating and finding its fulfillment in the majesty of the triune God. Turn your thoughts to the Lord and flee from even the mention of impurity.

Lord Jesus, help me to see the world through your eyes, that the actions of my heart would point to your creative purpose and design, and that I would joyfully see the beauty of your design and express them for your fame.

LOVE IS A PERSON

God is love.
1 JOHN 4:8 ESV

Love is not merely an affection, a concept, or a devotion; rather, it finds its grounding in the person and work of Jesus Christ. Our society communicates the essence of love as an emotive principle that is gauged by the individual, but the biblical account forges a different reality. Love is unified with truth in the person of Jesus. Christ entered the tapestry of creation full of grace and truth (John 1:14). He is the standard to which we are to grasp and understand the power of love.

Immerse yourself in the person of Christ and find yourself exemplifying the love that governs the universe. Suffuse yourself in the truth of the Scriptures and find yourself permeating the divine love of the triune God. For the Lord himself said, "If anyone loves me, he will keep my Word, and my Father will love him, and we will come to him and make our home with him" (John 14:23).

Lord Jesus, forgive me for chasing concepts and principles. Holy Spirit, help me to chase after Christ, that I would grow in my love and affections toward him.

RIGHTEOUSNESS OF CHRIST

Filled with the fruit of righteousness that comes through Jesus Christ, to the glory and praise of God.
PHILIPPIANS 1:11 ESV

A caricature of the Christian faith is rooted in a moralistic approach to the law. Though the Lord's commandments are important to the faith, they are not the entry point to which union with Christ is obtained. The grounds on which the saints will stand before an infinitely holy God are cemented not in a meritorious righteousness that is harbored innately, but through a righteousness that is found in Christ.

When we come to grips with the fact that our right standing with God is dependent upon Christ's fulfillment of the law, we will begin to walk in humility, not only toward the creator God (though that is amazingly wonderful) but also toward those we encounter daily. Your righteousness is not your own.

Lord, help me to yearn for your righteousness, that the outflow of my heart would be the righteousness that brings you glory.

MANNER OF LIFE

*Let your manner of life be
worthy of the gospel of Christ.*
PHILIPPIANS 1:27 ESV

One's belief system governs the external expression of life. Verbal commitments are shallow, even meaningless, without a proper response in conduct, commitment, and propriety. In actuality, the common thread that is produced in one's exterior engagement communicates a definitive posture of the heart.

The undergirding question then is, "What is informing one's belief system?" In order to properly establish a manner of life that is worthy of the gospel of Christ (Philippians 1:27), one must abide in his Word (John 15:4). Manner of life is not merely conduct from moment to moment, but a philosophy of living that is grounded in the gospel.

Lord Jesus, teach me to hunger for your Word, that the meditations of my heart would be saturated with your truth.

SUFFERING

It has been granted to you that for the sake of Christ you should not only believe in him but also suffer for his sake.
PHILIPPIANS 1:29 ESV

The tendency of this age is to question the Lord's goodness in the midst of suffering. Yet, from a biblical standpoint, suffering is the means by which the Lord conforms us into the image of the Son (Romans 8:29). When "bad" things happen in our lives, may we not ask, "Why me?" but rather, "What are you teaching me?"

If in Christ there is no condemnation (verse 1), then the suffering we face is not necessarily God's judgment. We can be assured that for those who love God all things work together for good, for those who are called according to his purpose (verse 28).

Lord Jesus, forgive me for pursuing my comfort over your glory. Teach me to walk in obedience, even if it means I must endure suffering. Help me to suffer well for your name.

HEART POSTURE

Do all things without grumbling or disputing.
PHILIPPIANS 2:14 ESV

As a believer of Jesus Christ, posture your heart in a manner that seeks to bring praise and honor to the Lord. As his child, put on his character and walk in his meekness. It should be your aim that in whatever you do, work heartily, as for the Lord and not for men (Colossians 3:23).

The intention of your heart is as important as the conduct of your behavior. Submit them both to his name.

Lord, incline my heart to your ways, that I may walk in contentment and serve in joy. May the posture of my heart be to see you glorified.

MORE OF HIM

That I may know him and the power of his resurrection,
and may share his sufferings,
becoming like him in his death.
PHILIPPIANS 3:10 ESV

Mimicking Jesus may not necessarily produce, from a worldly standpoint, the success that we are looking for. Yet reorienting our expectations and redefining advancement is necessary in seeing that the biblical definition of success is more about conformity to the image of Christ (Romans 8:29) and less about worldly recognition.

When we view the world through the gospel lens, we will find that trends do not dictate a faithful service to the Lord, but rather one's commitment to the biblical mandate of his disciples. In these scenarios, the Sunday school answer will never fail—Jesus!

Lord Jesus, teach me to see that you are my end goal. Sharpen my eyes to see that you are not a means to another end, but rather you are the end to my means.

COSTLY LOVE

*God shows his love for us
in that while we were still sinners,
Christ died for us.*
ROMANS 5:8 ESV

Love, service, and discipleship without cost do not resemble the biblical formation of gospel-saturated love. As the world continues to fight for convenience, may the saints of God embrace the sacrificial love that is personified through Jesus Christ.

The giving of yourself is posturing your heart in accordance with the Lord in order to convey the message of the gospel through deeds in service to others. In this way, you will mimic the creator God, who so loved the world, that he gave his only Son, that whoever believes in him should not perish but have eternal life (John 3:16).

Lord Jesus, forgive me when I serve you out of convenience. Remind me of how your call to discipleship is a call to death. Holy Spirit, help me see that Jesus is more valuable than my comfort.

ENDLESS SUPPLY

*He who did not spare his own Son but gave him up for us all,
how will he not also with him graciously give us all things?*
ROMANS 8:32 ESV

Discouragement, loneliness, and despair can find their way
into our lives. The one thing we can rest assured in during
those seasons of life is that our Lord is continuously faithful
to his people. The creator God did not hesitate in giving his
own Son on behalf of sinners in order to reconcile us back to
himself.

How much more will he give to us in our time of need? He
is an endless well of resources that brings forth life, vitality,
and security. When the world strips us of our pride, hope, and
assurance, he is the blanket that brings restoration to the soul.
We have a heavenly Father who is good to his children.

**Jesus, forgive me when I doubt the sufficiency of your
love. Your cross has displayed your love, and the
resurrection has proclaimed your faithfulness. Teach me
to trust that you hold me in your hand.**

DEBT OF LOVE

Owe no one anything, except to love each other,
for the one who loves another has fulfilled the law.
ROMANS 13:8 ESV

God demonstrated his love for us in that while we were still sinners, Christ died for us (Romans 5:8). This fact of divine love is a picture and a model to mimic, and it is to be paid forward, not for the merit of salvation but for the expression of gratitude. Service of love is in honor of the name that bought our salvation.

The Lord himself commissioned that we let our light shine before others, so that they may see our good works and give glory to our Father who is in heaven (Matthew 5:16).

Lord Jesus, I am in awe of your gift of salvation. Help me display your kindness. May the demonstration of your love draw people to the work of the Son by the power of the Spirit.

FUEL OF LOVE

We love because he first loved us.
1 JOHN 4:19 ESV

The extension of love in the Christian life finds its origin and fuel in the work and person of Jesus Christ. We love the poor because he was rich, yet for our sake he became poor, so that we by his poverty might become rich (2 Corinthians 8:9). We adopt because we have received the Spirit of adoption as sons, by whom we cry, "Abba! Father!" (Romans 8:15)

Our response in forgiveness is rooted in the fact that the call of Christ compels us to be kind to one another, tenderhearted, forgiving one another, as God in Christ forgave us (Ephesians 4:32). Christ is the fuel of love that empowers the soul!

Lord Jesus, grant me the power through your Spirit to extend the love with which you have loved me through the cross and resurrection. May your love shine forth from me to others today for your name's sake.

OUR PROVIDER

Abraham said, "God will provide for himself the lamb for a burnt offering, my son." So they went both of them together. So Abraham called the name of that place, "The LORD will provide"; as it is said to this day, "On the mount of the LORD it shall be provided."
GENESIS 22:8, 14 ESV

Abraham's actions seem like those of a mentally unstable father. God asked Abraham to do the unthinkable: to take his son and offer him up in sacrifice on Mt. Moriah. But something much deeper was going on in God's plan. You see, God was also foreshadowing a greater event. Abraham put the wood for the sacrifice on his son and hiked up to the place on the third day. The place? Moriah, which is only named one other time in the Bible (in 2 Chronicles 3:1), and it would be the place where King Solomon would build the temple one thousand years later.

Moriah was also near the place of Calvary, where God would sacrifice his only Son, Jesus, two thousand years later. Same place, wood to be sacrificed on, and something about the third day. Sound familiar? The pain of a father's heart was felt by the almighty God, who would offer up his own Son for our sin. Our biggest tests are the opportunities for God's biggest provisions.

Father God, give me faith to know that in the times of my biggest tests, you will always be there and provide me with everything I need.

PEACE

Laban said, "This heap is a witness between you and me today." Therefore he named it Galeed, and Mizpah, for he said, "The LORD watch between you and me, when we are out of one another's sight."
GENESIS 31:48-49 ESV

Laban and Jacob had a history. Jacob had asked to marry Laban's daughter, Rachel, but he was deceived by Laban and given her sister first, before he could marry the daughter he wanted. That was the start of a home filled with tension and jealousy. But God's blessing was on Jacob. Soon Jacob had twelve children. In his business he prospered in every way, and Laban became jealous. Distrust, resentment, and anger were starting to grow and infect their relationship. Finally, they gathered stones, not to throw at each other, but to build a memorial. They couldn't even agree on its name. Jacob called this memorial Mizpah, or watchtower. Here they agreed to disagree, and to submit to God together.

The fear of displeasing God became bigger than their disagreements with one another. They drew a line saying that their anger would go no further, and that they'd let the Lord watch between them. Finally, they celebrated with a feast and departed in peace. Sometimes conflicts are unavoidable. We may each have our list of reasons for the conflict. But like Jacob and Laban, we need a "Mizpah moment" where we agree to disagree and don't allow the conflict to get any worse.

God, may I not sin against you in my disagreements. Help me learn where to draw the line and when to leave the problem in your hands.

THE GOD WHO ANSWERS

God said to Jacob, "Arise, go up to Bethel and dwell there. Make an altar there to the God who appeared to you." So Jacob said to his household and to all who were with him, "Let us arise and go up to Bethel, so that I may make there an altar to the God who answers me in the day of my distress and has been with me wherever I have gone."

GENESIS 35:1-3 ESV

A terrible thing had happened to Jacob's family. Jacob had just moved his family back to Canaan when the son of a local ruler took Jacob's daughter and raped her (Genesis 34:2). The local ruler, Hamor, tried to fix things by arranging for his son to marry Dinah, the woman he had defiled. But Jacob's sons responded with vengeance, murdering the men of the town and then plundering the village (Genesis 34:25-29). Jacob's family was in chaos, and he felt a target on his own life for the violence of his sons.

When life seems out of control, what's a father to do? God called Jacob back to Bethel. Bethel was thirty miles south, but more importantly, it was the very place where Jacob had met God thirty years earlier when he pledged that the Lord would be his God (Genesis 28:19). When we have drifted away from God, he calls us back to himself.

Father, thank you that you will never give up on me. Refresh me and give me a new encounter with yourself. You are the God who answers in the day of my distress.

COUNTING OUR BLESSINGS

"The blessings of your father are mighty beyond the blessings of my parents, up to the bounties of the everlasting hills. May they be on the head of Joseph, and on the brow of him who was set apart from his brothers."

GENESIS 49:26 ESV

Jacob had lived a long life filled with a few high points but also much conflict. He lost the love of his life as she birthed their final son, Benjamin. He lost his son, Joseph, through a scheme of his other jealous sons who sold Joseph into slavery and deceived their father that he had been killed. When Jacob was later reunited with Joseph in Egypt, he reflected on his life before Pharaoh, calling his 130 years "few and unpleasant" and not living up to his fathers before him (Genesis 47:9). But seventeen years later, he assessed his life differently, saying that God had indeed blessed him, even more than his own parents.

What changed? Jacob began to count the rich mercies of God in his life. It's easy to encounter adversity and think our lives are without meaning. We can focus on people who disappoint us, work that is difficult, or a life that seems unfulfilled. Or we can focus on the many ways God has blessed us.

God, today I choose to be thankful. Today I will put aside my complaints and take time to remember your goodness in my life. Thank you for your faithfulness, your protection, and the many ways you demonstrate that you love me.

GUIDANCE

He said, "My presence will go with you, and I will give you rest." And he said to him, "If your presence will not go with me, do not bring us up from here."

EXODUS 33:14-15 ESV

Few would envy Moses and the task God called him to complete. Imagine leading millions of people for forty years through an uninhabited wilderness. Logistically, it took a miracle to provide food, water, and medical treatment for such a sizable and nomadic people. On top of this, the people were often filled with complaints and plots of rebellion. A three-day family road trip can be difficult enough. Imagine a forty-year trip!

Moses was wise enough to know what really mattered in life: to have God's presence in his life. God's presence includes his direction, protection, and blessing upon us and our families. Jesus told his disciples to abide in him, which meant to live in obedience and faithful relationship with him. God wants to be present with us. When God is present in our lives, there is rest and peace.

God, I thank you for the promise today that your presence will go with me and give me rest. May I faithfully follow you and enjoy your goodness in my life today.

COMPASSION, MERCY, GRACE

"The Lord, the Lord, a God merciful and gracious, slow to anger, and abounding in steadfast love and faithfulness, keeping steadfast love for the thousandth generation, forgiving iniquity and transgression and sin, yet by no means clearing the guilty, but visiting the iniquity of the parents upon the children and the children's children, to the third and the fourth generation."
Exodus 34:6-7 NRSV

Moses had a special relationship with God. God spared his life at birth, called him, told him what to say, and did many miracles through him. But what Moses really wanted was to be shown the glory of the Lord (Genesis 34:18), to see God. This was impossible, because the glory of the Lord is too great for us to see (verse 20). So God arranged an encounter where Moses would be hidden in the cleft of a rock as God's glory passed by. As the Lord passed, the first words he used to describe himself were that he is compassionate, merciful, and gracious. Have you found this to be true in your own life?

Have you known the compassion and grace of God in your own family? While God has a righteous standard—and the consequences of sin can be felt for three or four generations—the grace of God can be felt for a thousand generations.

Thank you, Father, for your compassion and mercy on me and my family. May my children, grandchildren, and even my future generations know how good you are.

STRONG AND BRAVE

"Joshua, be strong and brave! You must lead these people so they can take the land that I promised their fathers I would give them. Be strong and brave. Be sure to obey all the teachings my servant Moses gave you. If you follow them exactly, you will be successful in everything you do."

JOSHUA 1:6-7 NCV

Moses was dead, and Joshua was now being asked to do something that Moses was not asked to do. Yes, it took boldness and persistence for Moses to lead over six hundred thousand men (Numbers 2:23) plus the women, children, and uncounted Levites out of Egypt and travel through the Sinai Peninsula for forty years. Now the time had come to take the land that God originally promised to Abraham centuries earlier. Joshua would be entering a land filled with enemies and peril—no easy task. He was called to be strong, and that strength was based on two things: God's promise to be with him, and his own obedience in following God's commands (Joshua 1:5-6).

God is calling men to be strong today. Leadership is never easy. Like Joshua, our success depends on the same two things: God's promise to be with us, and our obedience to the God who calls us.

Thank you, Father, for the people you have brought into my life. You've called me today to be a godly influence. Remind me of your promises to be with me and never leave me. Strengthen me to obey you in all that you have commanded.

SUCCESS

"This Book of the Law shall not depart from your mouth, but you shall meditate in it day and night, that you may observe to do according to all that is written in it. For then you will make your way prosperous, and then you will have good success."

JOSHUA 1:8 NKJV

Joshua followed a successful leader, Moses. He had served as Moses' assistant (verse 1), a role that had both military and religious responsibilities. But more important than being Moses' right-hand man, Joshua was commissioned by God as leader of Israel, and the Lord promised to be with him (verse 5).

When God calls, he empowers us. When God calls, he promises success. Here God gives a clear roadmap to our success in life. What was true for Joshua as he led the armies of Israel is true for us today. Success comes from meditating on God's powerful written Word day and night. Meditating means reflecting on the Bible so it becomes part of our thoughts and values. Success is directly linked to the place of God's Word in both our thoughts and our actions each day.

God, you know how I'm easily distracted with many things throughout the day. Give me a desire to spend time in your Word. Give me a desire to search the Bible, because in it I find the secret to success.

VICTORY

"One of you routs a thousand, because the Lord your God fights for you, just as he promised. So be very careful to love the LORD your God."
JOSHUA 23:10-11 NIV

Joshua was now old and at the end of his life. He had fought many battles, and God gave Israel rest from their enemies. So Joshua called Israel together and recalled all their tremendous military success. He reminded them how the Lord had been fighting for them all along the way. Joshua also knew that life can get sloppy after a big win, that people can coast and forget to put God first. Now more than ever, they needed to be very careful to love the Lord God.

God is still fighting for us today. We face enemies of sin, including pride, lust, and greed. We have outside attacks on our health, our finances, and our business. We have family and loved ones who are being pressed by forces opposed to following God. But when God is fighting for us, amazing things happen. With God, we have the strength to rout a thousand enemies.

God, thank you for fighting for me and my loved ones. May my eyes be on you today, to love you and obey everything you have asked me to do. And most of all, may I remember that the battle is yours and you never fail.

SIGHT OF VISION

He answered, "Do not fear, for those who are with us are more than those who are with them." And Elisha prayed, and said, "LORD, I pray, open his eyes that he may see." Then the LORD opened the eyes of the young man, and he saw. And behold, the mountain was full of horses and chariots of fire all around Elisha.

2 KINGS 6:16-17 NKJV

Helen Keller was born without sight. She once said, "What is worse than being born without sight? Being born without vision!" Seeing and vision are not the same things. The prophet Elisha had vision but his servant did not. His servant could see only the Syrian king's army that surrounded Elisha at Dothan, ready to attack. It looked like Elisha and his servants were about to be destroyed. So Elisha prayed that his servant would "see" what God was doing. In God's hands they were completely safe.

We need vision to see what God is doing. Sometimes we are disappointed and discouraged. People let us down. Things don't turn out as we hoped. Resources appear slim. From our vantage point, there is little hope to cling to. But when God is at work, there is no reason to fear. Those with us are more than those who are with them.

God, give me your vision to see things your way. Open my eyes that I may see. Open my heart that I may love. Open my hands that I may help. Open my mind to understand the victories you have planned.

PRAISE

I will bless the LORD at all times;
his praise shall continually be in my mouth.
Oh, magnify the LORD with me,
and let us exalt his name together!
PSALM 34:1-3 ESV

For David, praise wasn't just a compliment to God. Instead, David's praise was an overflow of joy from a life made rich by God. As David wrote of God, his boasting was both continual and contagious (verse 3). He couldn't keep it to himself, wanting those around him to join him in praise. Each of us is different in how we express our praise. Praise may be loud or quiet. Sometimes it is spontaneous and erupts unhindered, and other times it is a slow, steady crescendo of being in awe of God's presence. Praise may be expressed as a simple "thank you, God" that wells up within.

C. S. Lewis wrote that we praise what we enjoy and that our praise doesn't just express our joy but completes our enjoyment of God. John Ortberg contrasts true praise against selfish pleasure and hedonism. With selfish pleasure, we demand more and more to please us, but then the law of diminishing returns kicks in and what made us happy yesterday no longer does today. Our capacity for joy declines. But with praise of God, the more we magnify the Lord, the more our praise expands. Our capacity for joy increases.

God, hear the praise of my heart today. May my delight in you resonate within me throughout my day. Remind me that my deep joy is only found in knowing you.

DELIVERANCE

I sought the LORD, and he answered me
and delivered me from all my fears.
Those who look to him are radiant,
and their faces shall never be ashamed.
This poor man cried, and the LORD heard him
and saved him out of all his troubles.
The angel of the LORD encamps around those who fear him,
and delivers them.
PSALM 34:4-7 ESV

David sought the Lord. King Saul wanted to kill David, so David ran to an enemy king, Abimelech, for protection (1 Samuel 21). To survive, David acted like a madman and Abimelech left him alone. Often in danger, David found deliverance in God. God delivered him from dreaded fears (verse 4) and many troubles (verse 6). God gave David answers, made him fearless, took away his shame, heard him, and saved him. David's deliverance began with him seeking the Lord.

Too often men spend their lives seeking things and the perfect circumstances. We grew up anticipating the next stage when life would be perfect: when I can drive, when I get a job, when I get a car, when I get married, when I have children, when I can retire, and on it goes. But there is never enough stuff, never the perfect life. However, when we seek the Lord, look for his direction, listen to his voice, and rejoice in his answers, he offers a profound sense of joy.

Father God, may I be known as a man who seeks you.
I need you and your deliverance today.

EXPERIENCE

Drink deeply of the pleasures of this God.
Experience for yourself the joyous mercies he gives
to all who turn to hide themselves in him.
Worship in awe and wonder, all you who've been made holy!
For all who fear him will feast with plenty.

PSALM 34:8-9 TPT

It takes time and practice to hear God; this is not for those of us in a hurry. Sometimes we encounter God the most when we are most desperate for him to come through and rescue us from trouble. I wish it wasn't that way, but God doesn't seem to mind, for he is always patient and full of lovingkindness. As we know God in the highs and lows of our everyday life, we discover just how good he is. For the writer of this psalm, the terror and dread of verse 4 that caused fear is replaced by the proper fear and reverence before God. The proper fear of God removes us from the fears of our daily life.

David wrote that the blessed person is the one who takes refuge in God (verse 8). Refuge is not found in the security of our investments, the authority of our job title, or even the devotion of our family and friends. Refuge is found in God. There is both joy and comfort when we step out and try God for ourselves. When we get a taste of the joy and goodness of God, both inner temptations and outer enemies lose their power against us. Those who taste, who drink deeply of God's presence and provision, will find their joy in him.

God, I'm ready to try something new. I'm ready to embark on a new adventure to see you work in my life. I want to experience more of you. You are good.

PREPARING FOR BLESSING

Know that the LORD, he is God!
It is he who made us, and we are his;
we are his people, and the sheep of his pasture.
PSALM 100:3 ESV

How does a man become blessed by God? We want God's blessing on our friendships, on our families, on our career, and on every aspect of our lives. This verse holds a key for unlocking the blessing of God. To be blessed by God, we must grasp three core realities. First, know who God is. Many misdirect their attention on knowing themselves, but there is greater value in knowing who God is. A. W. Tozer wrote that the most important thing about any man is what he thinks about God. When we know God, we find God alone is in charge; God is in sovereign control.

Second, know who made us. Back in 1859, Charles Darwin's Origin of the Species misled people to think there is no creator, but that we are just an evolved accident. How different to realize that God formed you and designed you in the image of himself with a purpose to live out. Third, know who leads us. Just like sheep, we are led by a Good Shepherd who knows us, guides us, provides for us, and protects us. This shepherd will one day lead us home to heaven.

God, you know the times when I've struggled with doubt, when I've wondered who I really am or even what I'm here for. I thank you that I have a shepherd, a good one, who has blessings planned for me as I follow your lead.

FAITH OR DOUBT

He said to Thomas, "Put your finger here, and look at my hands. Put your hand into the wound in my side. Don't be faithless any longer. Believe!" "My Lord and my God!" Thomas exclaimed.
JOHN 20:27-28 NLT

Depending on your background, you may have heard that having doubts about God is somehow a bad thing. One thing to recognize in the story of Thomas, is that Jesus never rebukes him for his doubt or turns him away. Jesus simply invites Thomas to touch him and then encourages him. Faith and doubt are almost always pitted against one another, but it may be better to see them as companions that complement one another. If you're having doubts about God or your ability to complete a certain task in your life, invite faith into the mental conversation as well. Consider that your doubt may actually be strengthening your faith.

It's okay to wrestle a little. We see it over and over in Scripture. Then, we also need to create a safe environment for other people to wrestle with things in their lives, whether it be their faith, questions about God, or just questions about life in general. Draw them in deeper, and don't turn them away. Ask them questions like, "Why do you think that?" Encourage them by saying, "That's a really good question. Tell me more about that."

God, I believe, but help my unbelief. Thank you for not shaming me when I have doubts.

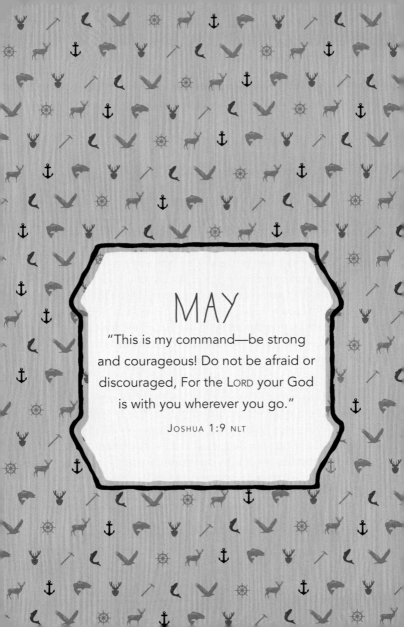

MAY

"This is my command—be strong
and courageous! Do not be afraid or
discouraged, For the LORD your God
is with you wherever you go."

JOSHUA 1:9 NLT

FEAR

"I, I am he who comforts you; who are you that you are afraid of man who dies, of the son of man who is made like grass, and have forgotten the LORD, your Maker, who stretched out the heavens and laid the foundations of the earth, and you fear continually all the day because of the wrath of the oppressor."

ISAIAH 51:12-13 ESV

Fear is a powerful force, and it can paralyze us from accomplishing the dreams God has for us. God allowed northern Israel to be defeated in 722 BC by the Assyrians for their unfaithfulness. In the south, Judah also stood in danger, as the king of Assyria threatened them also. But King Hezekiah of Judah took Isaiah's advice to pray to God, and Jerusalem was miraculously saved. God wanted his people to learn the lesson: the only way to conquer fear of man is to have a bigger fear: a healthy fear in God alone.

People who fear God need to fear nothing else. This fear of God includes a holy awe of who God is, a fear of disobeying him, and a fresh awareness of his power and plans for our lives. But when we fear people (verse 12), it demonstrates that we've forgotten God and his power (verse 13). John Calvin described fear as giving more power to the mortal man attacking you than to the power of God defending you.

Holy God, today I choose with your help to not fear others. Since you commanded me to not fear, I know you will also provide the power and resources I need to trust you. Today my heart is steadfast, trusting in you alone.

THE LORD'S PRAYER

"Give us this day our daily bread, and forgive us our debts, as we also have forgiven our debtors. And lead us not into temptation, but deliver us from evil."

MATTHEW 6:11-13 ESV

Jesus taught his followers to pray for what is already on his Father's heart. When we pray this, we are agreeing with God, who wants his name kept holy, his kingdom to be established, and his will to be done on earth just like it is done in heaven. Prayer is an attitude of the heart that humbles itself before God and cries out, "I need you!"

Jesus tells us to pray for ourselves in three areas, which is what God wants for us. First, we ask our Father to give us what we need, because he is a generous giver and delights in giving his children good gifts. As we inventory all we have, we recognize that everything has come from him. Second, we ask our Father to forgive us, because he knows there are thoughts we've had, words we've said, unkind things we've done, and love we've withheld. He is a gracious forgiver. He wants us to confess them and be restored with him. Third, we ask our Father to deliver us from temptation because he knows what we face each day. He is a mighty deliverer who will always rescue us when we ask.

You are a good Father! Thank you for your thoughts about me and that you know what I need. Thank you for inviting me to come before you and pray with confidence for these things. As I come to you, you transform me and allow me to trust you more.

FAMILY WORSHIP

Early the next morning they arose and worshiped before the LORD and then went back to their home at Ramah.
1 SAMUEL 1:19 NIV

Worship is important to the Father. Early in the morning, at the beginning of the week, it should become one of the very first acts that you do. It will set the spiritual tone for the rest of the week.

Here are a few suggestions to pull this off weekly:

- Ensure that you get plenty of rest the night before.
- Set out your clothes out for the next day.
- Wake up on time.
- If your pastor has shared what will be discussed, read that text during breakfast.
- Leave home in time to arrive ten minutes early.

When we make worship a personal priority by being prepared, we will grow to anticipate the activity of God. When we live in this humble expectation, we will look forward to worship.

Lord, I confess, I have not taken worshiping you as seriously as I ought. Help me view worship with the same importance as you do, and to ensure I see it as the priority for the week.

VISIONARY PRAYER

I pray that the eyes of your heart may be enlightened in order that you may know the hope to which he has called you, the riches of his glorious inheritance in his holy people, and his incomparably great power for us who believe.
EPHESIANS 1:18-19 NIV

Steve Jobs, the late cofounder of Apple, once said, "If you are working on something exciting that you really care about, you don't have to be pushed. The vision pulls you." Paul prayed that we'd have a God-shaped vision. He wanted us to see with our heart the hope, riches, and power God has for each one who believes. "Hope" expects God to fulfill what he promised. It doesn't live in limits, but instead lives in the realm of what God can do. "Riches" describes the believer's inheritance in Christ. All that Christ has is ours, and as we find promises in God's Word, we claim them in Christ.

But what good would it be to have wealth but be too weak to use it? So this God-shaped vision also includes power: the same power that rose Jesus from the dead. That power allows you to live with authority. Battles you face may try to intimidate, but greater is Jesus in you than anything in the world.

God, I need your vision to live with the hope, riches, and power you have for me. Pull me through today with this God-shaped vision.

RECREATED

You are no longer strangers and aliens, but you are fellow citizens with the saints and members of the household of God, built on the foundation of the apostles and prophets, Christ Jesus himself being the cornerstone.

EPHESIANS 2:19-20 ESV

In Christ, everything has changed. Once Israel was God's only chosen nation, but now the people in Christ are. He has re-created us as fellow citizens. Once we were strangers to the things of God, but now we are members of God's family, adopted as full members of God's household. In the Old Testament days, non-Jews couldn't go into the temple area, but now we are being re-created as a holy temple to the Lord where his Spirit lives (verse 21).

What does this all mean? First, we look at ourselves differently. Habits, memories, fears, and past things need no longer control us, because we have been brought near to God. Second, we look at others differently. Judgment no longer comes pouring out of our mouths. We've been forgiven and are grateful. The blueprint has been written, and the Master Builder is following his plan in re-creating us according to new specs. The cornerstone marked the start of the foundation the builder would use so the building was square and true. In this new plan, Jesus Christ is the cornerstone, and all that is built will be true and according to God's plan.

Father, thank you for what you are creating in me. Thank you that I am no longer an outsider, but an insider in your family.

WALKING IN LOVE

Be imitators of God, as beloved children. And walk in love, as Christ loved us and gave himself up for us, a fragrant offering and sacrifice to God.
EPHESIANS 5:1-2 ESV

What an audacious statement. How could someone possibly imitate God? And how could one possibly ask us to be imitators of God? Doesn't the whole idea sound ridiculous? The secret to this whole idea is found in the phrase "as beloved children." This is more than a kind expression. The original wording points to both the character and reason for that imitation. We are to be like God because we are his children. Can you think of some way you are like your dad? Maybe you have your dad's voice, his smile, his walk, his sense of humor, or his keen wit. He didn't have to teach you; as his son, you naturally resemble him in some way.

There are ways we'll never be like God, but we are to imitate him in one way: how we love. Jesus was both our example and the cause of this new ability. Because of what Jesus did, we have a new ability to love others around us. There's little room for complaining how hard it is to love another person because it is the love of Jesus, not our own, that we're giving.

Father, thank you for designing me to love like Jesus loves. It's now in my spiritual DNA. May your love leak out of me today, especially to those who have been hard for me to love. Thank you for making me your child. Maybe someday people will look at me and be drawn to you.

POWER

Be filled with the Spirit, addressing one another in psalms and hymns and spiritual songs, singing and making melody to the Lord with your heart, giving thanks always and for everything to God the Father in the name of our Lord Jesus Christ, submitting to one another out of reverence for Christ.

EPHESIANS 5:18-21 ESV

When we became Christians, the Holy Spirit was given to us (1 Corinthians 12:13). Paul wrote to Christians who had the Spirit, but said they needed to be filled with that Spirit. He wasn't saying they needed more of the Spirit, but that the Spirit needed more of them. As we yield our will, our plans, and our self to God, the Holy Spirit can take control and lead us.

How do we know if we aren't filled? We may see conflict in our relationships, our prayer life may seem stale, we may be living a double life of tension between our old self and new life in Christ, or people around us may not be seeing the evidence of the Spirit in us (love, joy, peace, patience, kindness, goodness, faithfulness, gentleness, and self-control; Galatians 5:22-23). If any of this is true, we need to ask God to fill us with the Holy Spirit. Jesus reminded us that our heavenly Father will give the Holy Spirit to those who ask him (Luke 11:13).

Father God, I don't want just an experience; I desire you. Fill me with your Holy Spirit today. I don't want to live in my own strength alone; I need you. I want to love you with all my heart, soul, mind, and strength, and I want the Spirit of Christ to fill me completely.

ARMOR AND STRENGTH

Be strong in the Lord and in the strength of his might.
Put on the whole armor of God, that you may be able to stand
against the schemes of the devil.
EPHESIANS 6:10-11 ESV

At some point, we discover that life is more like a battleground than a playground. We encounter tests and tough times and may even feel like we're under attack. As Paul wrote the words above, he was in prison in Rome and felt discouraged and isolated. He knew men needed to gain strength from the Lord. Battle-time living forces us to be alert, strategic, and focused. We understand there are false ideas in our cultures that attack our values. We look within and know our old nature can rise up and resist the things of God. The Bible also reveals that there is a devil with schemes against men who follow God.

But God does not leave us defenseless in this battle. God gives us armor to wear: weapons of truth, righteousness, peace, faith, salvation, and God's Word (verses 13-18). Martin Luther wrote *A Mighty Fortress is our God,* including the words, "although this world with devils filled should threaten to undo us, we will not fear for God has willed his truth to triumph through us." God has plans for your success. In Christ, you have a champion: the Lord, mighty in battle.

Lord, mighty in battle, show your strength in my life today. Protect those I love. Show me how to stand in your strength. Thank you that the enemies around me are no match for you, my Savior.

LIVING BY FAITH

Without faith it is impossible to please him, for whoever would draw near to God must believe that he exists and that he rewards those who seek him.

HEBREWS 11:6 ESV

What is faith, and why is living by faith so difficult? Here we see that the requirements of true faith are contrary to life in our world. Faith is not blind. Faith is based on real evidence that most people reject without testing: evidence that Jesus resurrected from the dead and that there is a real God who exists, created everything, and has demonstrated love to us.

Faith taps into God's story, which is more real than the story of our natural world. God's story starts, "In the beginning, God" and ends with Jesus saying, "I am coming quickly," and is written in four acts. The first act is God's creation where everything was good. The second act was the fall to sin and the sentence of hard work, sorrow, and death. The third act began immediately after the fall in the garden as God unfolded his plan to redeem the people he created from their sin. The final act, pictured in Revelation, includes God re-creating a new heaven and earth and restoring all. To believe in God is to live in his story, where he rewards those who seek him. Living by faith is the only way we can please God.

God, thank you for your story. Life can wear me down, and sometimes it seems like I'm stuck in the second act: hard work, sorrow, and death. Remind me that your story is at work. By your help, I will live by faith in you and your story today.

FAITH IN GOD'S PLAN

The power of faith prompted Isaac to impart a blessing to his sons, Jacob and Esau, concerning their prophetic destinies.
HEBREWS 11:20 TPT

Abraham's son Isaac had to live by faith throughout his life. The birth of Isaac's twin sons, Jacob and Esau, was no ordinary birth. In Genesis 25:23, the Lord said to their expectant mother, Rebekah, that two nations were in her womb and the older would serve the younger. Isaac loved Rebekah, but each favored a different one of the twins.

The verse above portrays the closing event of Isaac's life. As Isaac prepared to give the inheritance to the older, preferred Esau, Rebekah and Jacob intervened and gained the inheritance by deceit. When Isaac discovered that the "wrong son" gained the inheritance, he did not try to undo his action. By faith he stepped into God's plan of blessing even when it went against his own. Isaac realized there was a bigger story at work, and he determined to live by God's plan and not his own. Each of us is called to live by faith. What does that look like in your life? Is there something God has asked you to do, even if it goes against your own plans and desires? Isaac lived "regarding things to come." And that life of faith made all the difference.

Father, help me to live by faith in you this week. I realize there are times when I only want to do what I want to do, and I can make my decisions based only on what I see and what benefits me. Thank you for calling me to live in your bigger story.

MENTORING

Remember your leaders,
those who spoke the word of God to you;
consider the outcome of their way of life,
and imitate their faith.

HEBREWS 13:7 NRSV

As men, we're never alone. We grow by observing the examples of others, and each of us needs someone to lead us. Hebrews 11 gives a long list of courageous heroes who have stood strong in the faith, and each generation has more faith-filled leaders for us to learn from. We observe how they live and how they show faith that is rock solid. We watch how they make decisions, how they love as men, how they pray, how they handle finances, and how they face conflict. We watch so we can follow and be stronger ourselves.

To stand strong, we also need someone to walk alongside us. We need a brother to pray with and share with as we grow together in faith. We're also part of the passing of the baton of faith to the next generation. That means we need to invest our lives and our faith in a younger man.

Father God, I thank you for the godly men in my life. May I remember their lives and imitate their faith. I pray that others see the same faith in me to follow.

WISDOM FROM ABOVE

If anyone longs to be wise, ask God for wisdom and he will give it! He won't see your lack of wisdom as an opportunity to scold you over your failures but he will overwhelm your failures with his generous grace.

JAMES 1:5 TPT

When Solomon began his reign as king in Israel, he prayed to God for one thing: wisdom (1 Kings 3). God was pleased that he didn't ask for long life, riches, or vengeance on his enemies. Solomon asked for the most important thing. So God rewarded him, giving him a discerning heart like no other. God then blessed Solomon with riches and honor in addition to the wisdom.

Each of us faces trials and challenges where our own human understanding is not enough. We don't see the answer. We don't have the resources. Maybe something unexpected has happened. Maybe our best plans didn't work out. Maybe there is a conflict with someone, and we don't see the way out. We need God's wisdom. The good news is that God tells us to ask for wisdom, and that he will give it if we ask. And God is not stingy but generous in giving us wisdom.

Father, thank you for your wisdom. You know the challenges I am facing right now. I need you to get me through this. I thank you that you are a generous Father, and I trust you now.

STEADFAST

Let what you heard from the beginning abide in you.
If what you heard from the beginning abides in you,
then you too will abide in the Son and in the Father.
1 JOHN 2:24 ESV

If you have ever replaced a light fixture, you know you have to connect the black wires and white wires to each other. The hot wire supplies the power, and a neutral wire carries that current back. But the third wire is very important. Electricity is always looking for the shortest path back to the earth, so if there is a problem, the third wire—the grounding wire—provides a direct path back to the ground, preventing you from becoming that shortest path and suffering serious shock.

Some people live life without the ground wire attached. When the unexpected happens, we need to be grounded. John wrote that we need to abide in Christ. What was so clear to us when we were younger can become unclear and confusing. Remembering what we have learned and experienced in Jesus allows us to remain grounded and unshakeable when life gets stormy.

Father God, make me unshakeable. I remember a time when things seemed more clear. May Jesus be my anchor point, my grounding wire today.

FAMILY

See what kind of love the Father has given to us, that we should be called children of God; and so we are. The reason why the world does not know us is that it did not know him.

1 JOHN 3:1 ESV

Here is an amazing truth: In Christ we are part of God's family. Everyone is God's creation, but the Bible is clear that those who have received the Son are the ones who are called children of God (John 1:12). The first word, *see* or *behold*, is a sharp command to pay attention because something marvelous is about to be said. The title is real, so John adds here "and so we are."

We are God's family. God hasn't just forgiven us; he has also given us himself. As children, we stand in a unique and certain position. We have a legal position defining our status as part of God's family. We are heirs, we have access to come boldly into our Father God's presence in prayer, and we can know His love every day.

Father God, I am amazed that you have made me your child. You have placed me in your family. You have forgiven me, and your thoughts of me are wonderful. I will live in the joy and honor of the family name today.

FUTURE

Beloved, we are God's children now, and what we will be has not yet appeared; but we know that when he appears we shall be like him, because we shall see him as he is.

1 JOHN 3:2 ESV

There's a future event that God's children look forward to: the return of Jesus. In 1 John 2:28 and 3:2, John uses two words to describe this: Jesus' *coming* and his *appearance*. In the Roman Empire, when a ruler visited, there was great celebration and rejoicing. Here, we read of Jesus' appearance that we will see. Jesus said he will return when the Father decides, and when all peoples have heard (Matthew 24:14).

When Jesus returns, we will be changed. In Christ, we already have been changed to have a new nature, to be aware when we sin, and to have a desire to live for God. But when Jesus returns, the change will be complete because we are destined for glory. We will be like him because we will see him as he is, face-to-face.

Lord Jesus, I rejoice that you are coming again. I don't understand everything about that great event, but I take comfort that I am your child, and you have a great future planned for me.

SHOWING GOD'S LOVE

*Little children, let us not love in word or talk
but in deed and in truth.*
1 JOHN 3:18 ESV

Love, for a child of God, is not just a duty but a way of knowing who you are. The preacher Martyn Lloyd-Jones observed that in the New Testament, we are never called to do anything without first being reminded of who we are. And because of Christ, we love. We don't make ourselves Christians by showing love; we show that we are Christians by our love.

There may be some people who you don't like very much. Maybe they are negative, mean, pushy, lazy, thoughtless, insulting, or irritating. But this is different. Loving isn't based on our personality differences or whether or not we like the other person. Because God is love (1 John 4:8) and we are God's children, we love. And love is not an idea or a soft, sentimental feeling. Love must express itself. Who will you show God's love to today?

Father, you are love. You made me to love. May I live out your design in me today.

OVERCOMERS

Little children, you are from God and have overcome them,
for he who is in you is greater than he who is in the world.
1 JOHN 4:4 ESV

At the end of the first century, John wrote to Christians who had much to fear. Christians lived a fragile existence that found few comforts in daily life, and they were persecuted by Jewish Zealots and then the Roman government, which often made Christians scapegoats for national problems. As well, false teachers twisted truths about Jesus and the Christian life. John wanted the Christians to know who they were (from God) and the power they had.

Overcoming is natural in the life of the believer. We overcome when we don't give up in our faith, when we refuse to live in fear, and when we continue to obey when others around us don't. We overcome when we remember that the Jesus in us is greater than any force in the world. Victory is certain when we remain in Christ.

Lord Jesus, thank you that because of you I am an overcomer. You know my situation today. I claim this truth that you are greater than any force I face. In you my victory is certain.

SACRAMENTAL PEOPLE

Beloved, if God so loved us,
we also ought to love one another.
1 JOHN 4:11 ESV

Love is one of those subjects that is easy to talk about but difficult to put into practice. It was said that twentieth-century theologian Karl Barth was asked what the greatest theological truth was, and he replied, "Jesus loves me this I know, for the Bible tells me so." On a cold, winter's day, your dog delights in curling up in front of the fire and soaking in the warmth. God's love is like that. It does no good to think about the concept of love; we have to soak it in and let its warmth penetrate us, so we can love others.

A sacrament is a means of grace, a channel of God's grace to us. Greg Ogden uses the term "sacramental people." We are to be God's sacraments to others, the channel by which they feel the warmth of his love. Once Jesus was asked what the greatest commandment was, and he responded to love God and our neighbor as ourselves. When he was asked about the neighbor, Jesus dialed up the discussion and gave the story of the Samaritan who showed love to the man attacked by thieves. Love gets down to the nitty-gritty details of reaching out to people's needs. And when we do that, we are a sacrament, a channel of God's love to others.

Father, I thank you that you are love and you designed me to love others. Show me who you want me to love today. May others see how loving you are based on my actions.

FEARLESS

There is no fear in love, but perfect love casts out fear.
For fear has to do with punishment,
and whoever fears has not been perfected in love.
1 JOHN 4:18 ESV

Did John say "perfect"? Can you ever imagine telling a family member or close friend, "Yes, I'm perfect in the way I love"? John isn't writing that we are now perfect, but that we are being completed and developed as we reach for our intended goal as God designed us to be. We've been designed to love. Before we knew Christ, we were designed to respond to someone in the same way they treated us. If someone pushed us, we'd push back a little harder. But the new design is quite an upgrade. The Christ in us does not respond like that; in fact, we show love to those who don't love us first.

This new love makes us fearless. We are fearless as we face death, and we are fearless as we face everyday life. The key to living without fear is to have a greater power that drives out fear. That greater power is the love of God. Consider the dad who would run into a burning house to rescue his child trapped in there. The love for that child is greater than the fear of that fire. God's love makes us fearless.

Father, I thank you for your love. Remind me who I am. I don't need to live in fear because the God of the universe loves me. I no longer fear your judgment since you love me. Make me fearless today.

CONFIDENCE

This is the confidence that we have toward him,
that if we ask anything according to his will he hears us.
1 JOHN 5:14 ESV

Men are expected to be confident. If we don't believe
in ourselves, then who will? But, what does that confidence
look like? Fake it until you make it? Speak louder than the
other guy? There's a quiet confidence shown by the man of
God. Bluster and acting confident will only go so far. The
apostle John spoke of a different kind of confidence. This is
confidence not based on our performance, but in the one who
sent his Son, called us his children, and promised us eternal
life. He has called us to come into his presence boldly and to
pray with confidence.

When we pray confidently, we enter the throne room
of heaven, the universe's largest arena. As men, we bring
ourselves, and especially those who depend on us. Our
families, our friends, and our coworkers need us to be
confident in prayer. And when we pray, because we are his
children, we know that God hears us.

God, thank you for inviting me to come into your presence
every day. Help me to pray bold prayers filled with faith
because people in my life need me. Thank you for your
promise that if I pray, you'll listen.

DREAMING AGAIN

*When the LORD restored the fortunes of Zion,
we were like those who dreamed.*
PSALM 126:1 NIV

Life has a way of stealing, crushing, and shrinking our dreams. There was a time when our dreams motivated us, stirred our hearts, and fueled passion in our souls. We were small, but our dreams were huge. The writer of Psalm 126 reminds us that it is never too late to dream again. After a generation of captivity in Babylon, God set his people free. They were free to return home, and they were free to dream again. Not just set free but set free to dream.

A new season is a great opportunity to dream again, to rediscover old dreams and to ask God to give us new ones. When you consider God's faithfulness, his trustworthy character, and his call to adventure, asking him to give us new dreams seems a small thing for his big heart. Be courageous and invite God to give you a renewed ability to dream again.

God, you showed your faithfulness to your people, restoring them and giving them a new dream. In this new season in my life, I invite you do this incredible work in my heart. Let me dream again. Release your great big dreams into my life today.

LAUGHING AGAIN

Our mouths were filled with laughter, our tongues with songs of joy. Then it was said among the nations, "The Lord has done great things for them." The Lord has done great things for us, and we are filled with joy.

PSALM 126:2-3 NIV

When was the last time you laughed at the ridiculous, scandalous, and radical love of God expressed in Jesus Christ? Consider for a few moments the impact of your experience. Laughter and joy are a witness to the work of God in our lives. The psalmist makes this point with incredible, exaggerating language. The very nations will declare the goodness of God when they see your expressed joy.

Men, imagine the impact we could make on our communities if we began to discover the power of laughter and joy. If nations can be impacted by the joyful return of God's people to Jerusalem, surely our emotional energy can impact our city. Maybe if we can tap into joy and begin to laugh again—if we can open our mouths and express ourselves in worship—just maybe our neighbors might declare, "The Lord has done great things for them."

God, remind me today of your incredible saving work in my life. Let the power of your love overflow and overwhelm me. Fill my heart with joy and my mouth with praise and help me to display my joy to my world.

FINDING HOPE AGAIN

Those who sow with tears will reap with songs of joy.
Those who go out weeping, carrying seed to sow,
will return with songs of joy, carrying sheaves with them.
PSALM 126:5-6 NIV

God takes his time to accomplish his work. It's frustrating but true. As busy men, we sometimes wish he would pick up the pace. Then we remember how carefully, intentionally, and graciously he is doing his transforming work in our lives, and we remember that his timing is perfect. He really understands his children.

The writer of Psalm 126 understood two things. He understood farming, and so he understood that timing is everything. Preparing, planting, caring, watching, and reaping—everything has a season. But the writer also understood that with God's deep transforming work, a spiritual miracle is needed. If a farmer sows tears, then it would stand to reason that he would reap tears. As we work in partnership with God's perfect timing, our reward is lasting change. We might sow in tears, but at harvest time the fruit of those tears will be revealed in powerful joy.

God, I wait on you to do your powerful transforming work in my heart. I long to grow again. I hope for a new season, one where lasting change takes place in my life. Give me patience to trust your timing and give me commitment to your processes.

LIGHT SHINES IN

The people who walked in darkness
have seen a great light;
those who lived in a land of deep darkness—
on them light has shined.

ISAIAH 9:2 NRSV

Common sense is overrated. It's not bad; it's just overrated. God calls people to trust him deeply and radically, and even to follow him at the expense of common sense. Faith is our ability to trust God right now, today, in this moment. Hope is our ability to trust God for the future. That's hard. Isaiah's message was one of incredible hope. Just a few chapters before the words above were unleashed, the prophet was explaining to God's people that they had chosen darkness as their path. Their rebellious hearts and their consistent disobedience had led them down a path of darkness. The prophet might say it this way: "I think you are lost."

That sounds a lot like our friends or family members when we get lost on a road trip. It's hard to admit it, but the person sitting beside us is usually right. But there is hope. In the car we call it Google Maps, and in our faith journey we call him Jesus. He comes to illuminate our lostness and to gently lead us back into his perfect plan. Common sense says figure it out yourself. But Jesus says he is the light of the world (John 8:12; 9:5).

God, let your light shine in my heart today. Illuminate my ways. Help me to trust you radically and fix my eyes on you for the future.

WANDERING SOUL

All of us, like sheep, have strayed away.
We have left God's paths to follow our own.
Yet the LORD laid on him the sins of us all.
ISAIAH 53:6 NLT

Something is broken inside of us, and as men we know it. We watch the people in our lives as they struggle to keep in line with the values and vision of God. Truthfully though, we know something is broken from looking inside ourselves. We are prone to wander. We see it in others, but more importantly we feel it in our own journey with Christ. The prophet Isaiah described this predicament by using an image from the world of shepherding. He was speaking to the elders of God's people, known as the shepherds of the flock. He reminds them that they were no different from the people they had been called to shepherd.

What an amazing encouragement! If godly men who are called and empowered as leaders struggle to walk on God's path, I think we can stop beating ourselves up. Instead we can lean into truth. Here is one incredible theological truth: Jesus did not wander from the path. He was committed to his journey to the cross and to his substitutionary death. Now, no matter how many times we find ourselves wandering from God's path, we can, through Christ's power, find our way back to the flock and to a restored soul.

Thank you, Lord, for being my shepherd, for giving me all I need. Guide me along your paths day by day.

FOLLOWING FOR OTHERS

Be imitators of me, as I am of Christ.
1 CORINTHIANS 11:1 ESV

Have you ever had the sneaky suspicion that you were being watched? Well you are! Is it your creepy neighbor, your suspicious boss, or the mailman? It's all of them, and many, many more.

When Paul spoke the above words to his church family in Corinth, he was inviting them to intentionally watch and copy his life in Christ. He was learning to follow Jesus and was living openly for all to see so that they could follow. Men, live your faith out loud for others to see, to copy, to follow, and to become.

God, help me follow you in such a way that those who are following me see you and see Jesus.

IN MY PLACE

God made him who had no sin to be sin for us,
so that in him we might become the righteousness of God.
2 CORINTHIANS 5:21 NIV

Have you ever had to tackle a really messy job?
Perhaps you decided to wash your car by hand or bathe
a rambunctious dog to prevent him from tracking mud
throughout the house. If you aren't careful you may find that
while your car or dog will be clean and shiny due to your
efforts, you will now be the messy one.

The apostle Paul uses a similar illustration to help his
church understand the amazing work of Christ on our behalf.
Jesus entered our messy lives and took all that mess onto
himself. This transaction left us clean, pure, perfect, and holy.
Christ makes us completely righteous before God, while he,
on the cross, hangs in the darkness of our sin and shame.
Our mess becomes his mess. His perfect nature becomes our
perfect nature. What an amazing work.

**God, thank you for Jesus, my Savior and my substitute.
Thank you that he enters my messy story and takes all
that is mine and makes it his and gives me all that is his.
I'm in awe. Thank you for this incredible work.**

GENEROUS WITH IDENTITY

Even before he made the world, God loved us and chose us in Christ to be holy and without fault in his eyes. God decided in advance to adopt us into his own family by bringing us to himself through Jesus Christ. This is what he wanted to do, and it gave him great pleasure.
EPHESIANS 1:4-5 NLT

There is something about being a dad and being generous. Did your dad ever bring you a gift when he got back from a road trip? Or perhaps he slipped you a dollar or two to purchase that candy bar you were drooling over while waiting in line at the grocery store? It is such an enjoyable thing, for both you and your dad!

In Ephesians 1:5, the apostle Paul expresses God's father heart by explaining that he gave his children something that "gave him great pleasure." As we receive gifts from our heavenly Father, he experiences pleasure in our receiving them. Verse 4 explains that on this occasion, God's gift to us is the gift of belonging. We are in his family. We are his children. Generosity seems to work in two ways. We get to give gifts to others while we ourselves receive the pleasure of being generous. Perhaps the most incredible gift we can give to the people in our lives is the gift of our time and attention.

God, thank you for your generous heart. Help me to also be a generous gift giver today. May I recognize that it truly is better to give than it is to receive.

I NEED MORE

He is so rich in kindness and grace that he purchased our
freedom with the blood of his Son and forgave our sins.
EPHESIANS 1:7 NLT

I think every man wishes he had more to give. More money, more time, more talent, more heart, and more energy. We're all giving all we have, but the issue is capacity. There are limits to our output. What if there was another source to tap into? A limitless reservoir that could provide all we need for our calling as men.

Ephesians 1:7 gives us a beautiful picture of God's capacity. He is so rich. He is rich in kindness and rich in grace. He has so much kindness and so much grace that he was able to purchase our forgiveness and redemption from the slave market of sin. This verse also gives us an idea of the depths of resources available to us. We might have a limit to our kindness and a very real limit to our grace, but our heavenly Father has an abundance, and he is clearly willing to share it with us.

God, when I run out of capacity, when my ability to show kindness and grace to my friends and family is extended to the limit, help me tap into your great big heart and abundant resources.

SAFE AND SECURE

When you believed in Christ, he identified you as his own by giving you the Holy Spirit, whom he promised long ago. The Spirit is God's guarantee that he will give us the inheritance he promised and that he has purchased us to be his own people.
EPHESIANS 1:13-14 NLT

Often in our journey as men, we get a little lost. Those crazy moments when we're sure it was supposed to be a left, left, then right; yet we find ourselves at a dead end. Oops! We also get lost in ourselves. We lose our sense of identity. We are so busy driving around, working, shopping, and investing in friendships. Along the way, we forget that we have a greater identity. Before we are a man, a friend, or an employee, before we belong to the system, the rat race, or the coaching team, we belong to God.

We might feel lost, but we are not lost. He has placed inside of us a gift of security. His Holy Spirit has found his way into our heart and has taken up permanent residence. His job is to transform us, to equip us and unleash us, and to also just to remind us. The apostle Paul tells us that the Spirit is God's guarantee that he will give us the inheritance he promised. In simple terms, the Spirit is the down payment that secures us into the contract. We might lose our way and our sense of who we are along the way, but we cannot lose our place among the purchased people of God. We belong to him.

God, let your Spirit speak to my spirit today. Remind me of your place in my heart. Awaken my soul to your Holy Spirit and call me back to Jesus again.

IDENTITY AND CALLING

This letter is from Paul, chosen by the will of God to be an apostle of Christ Jesus. I have been sent out to tell others about the life he has promised through faith in Christ Jesus.
2 TIMOTHY 1:1 NLT

As men, one of our greatest challenges is staying focused. There's always so much background noise! And we can find ourselves running from crisis to crisis or from activity to activity. Who are we, what has God called us for, and what is our role as a man? If we can keep our eyes on the vision, then all the little things make more sense.

When the apostle Paul introduced himself in 2 Timothy, he wasn't speaking to the church but to himself. He was locked in a prison, awaiting his execution, missing his friends, and hurting from the pain of his ministry journey. Yet his words sound like a rallying call. He was rallying himself for one final push toward the finish line, no matter what was happening in the background. So he reminded himself of his identity and mission in Christ. Who are you, and what are you called to be and do?

God, speak to me today. Speak to my identity, speak to my calling. Remind me of the big picture and help me focus my heart on it.

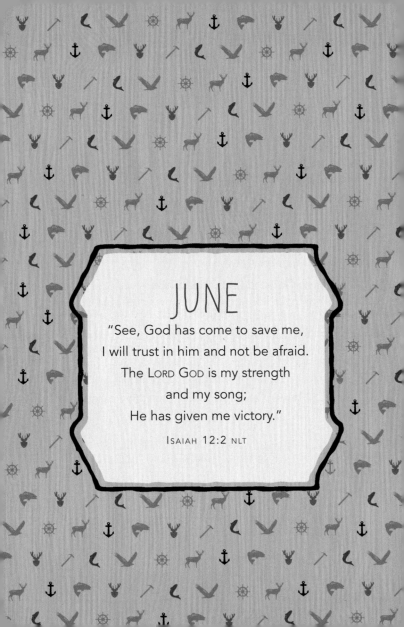

JUNE

"See, God has come to save me,
I will trust in him and not be afraid.
The LORD GOD is my strength
and my song;
He has given me victory."

ISAIAH 12:2 NLT

COMMITTED

"Come," he replied,
"and you will see."
JOHN 1:39 NIV

No doubt you didn't know everything about your best friend the day you met, and you most likely don't know everything about him or her right now. That's kind of how people work. There are layers and stories that gradually get exposed over time. We grow in our knowledge of each other over time, and over the years a close friend's actions and thoughts become predictable.

This same pattern exists with God. When Jesus invited his first followers to journey with him, he didn't say, "Here's a one-million-page contract and explanation offering everything you need to know about what you're stepping into." Nope. Instead, he said, "Come, and you will see." The same is true with us. No one knows everything there is to know about God; that's part of the journey. But as we take steps after Jesus, we begin to see how predictable his kindness is and how reliable his provisions are. Today he may be inviting you to another day of trusting him, another day of coming and seeing.

God, I am committed to the journey, and I know that you are committed to me. I will come and see what you have for me today!

HUMILITY

This was his message:
"After me comes the one more powerful than I."
MARK 1:7 NIV

Can you imagine Time magazine with a man on the cover and a quote at the bottom saying, "I don't have the answer. I'm not the solution"? It sounds far-fetched, doesn't it? How about an author who says, "I really don't have what you need. Wait for the one who follows me. He's the one you really need to check out"? Again, hard to imagine. Still, that's a rough parallel to one of John the Baptist's central messages: "After me comes the one more powerful than I." That was a remarkable thing to say, especially since everyone from the city and the countryside was hanging on his every word (Mark 1:5).

John the Baptist set an example for contemporary followers of Jesus. It's easy for us to get sucked up into the "look at me, notice me" approach that is often pushed in our culture. But John the Baptist resisted the pull of self-promotion because he wasn't focused on the adoring crowds or his own eloquence but on the one who would come after him. Humility happens when our focus is on "the one more powerful than I."

Father, rid me of my toxic and insecure self-focus. Help me to live focused on you. Give me your strength so I might love your world.

OPEN UP

How long, LORD, must I call for help,
but you do not listen?
HABAKKUK 1:2 NIV

Pain happens. Whether it's the physical pain of an injury, the emotional pain of a fractured relationship, or the unexplained hurt of an accident, pain has a habit of working its way into our life. Often, trying to convince ourselves that everything will get better doesn't help (and it's even worse if a friend tells us that). The most pressing issue is the pain, and to assert optimism early proves unconvincing.

The Bible, rather than prodding us with Hallmark-esque naïveté, speaks with stark honesty. Habakkuk, for example, shares his broken heart with God, and he doesn't hold back. Throughout his exchange with God, he gradually finds himself content, even without all his hopes fulfilled. But that doesn't happen quickly, and, even more importantly, it only happens when Habakkuk is completely open and honest with God. It's only when we dare to ask God the tough questions about pain and confusion that he can begin to heal and transform us.

God, search me to see if I am hiding pain or confusion that I should be sharing with you. I do have hurt and questions. Will you be my guide in this troubling situation?

WORKERS

Then he said to his disciples,
"The harvest is plentiful but the workers are few.
Ask the Lord of the harvest, therefore,
to send out workers into his harvest."
MATTHEW 9:37-38 NIV

In the face of the great need for workers, Jesus didn't mount a marketing campaign, craft an elevator pitch, or hire a consultant. Instead, he said that we should "ask the Lord of the harvest." This goes against our instinct. In the face of great need, it makes sense to send out e-mails and make phone calls, saying, "Please?"

Jesus says that we should pray for workers as a first step because God is the Lord of the harvest. That means he's in control. Jesus is inviting his followers to acknowledge that prayer is the first and most important step, even as the world is filled with overwhelming needs. This of course doesn't mean that the actions of evangelism, service, and social justice aren't important; they're vital. It just means that the priority is to ask the Lord of the harvest to provide for the need.

Father, I acknowledge that you are the Lord of the harvest. Send workers to address the needs around the world and in my city.

RESET MY SOUL

*In the beginning God created
the heavens and the earth.*
GENESIS 1:1 NIV

We experience our pain and problems differently when we understand who is in control and trust the process he pulls us through. We have an important role to play in our lives, but the hero in our story is not us.

The words of Genesis 1:1 echo throughout Scripture as a reminder of who has been in control since the beginning. Mark 1:1, John 1:1, and 1 John 1:1 all remind us of the need to reset our soul and put our trust in the one who set creation in motion. Issues in our lives can pull us away from God's presence. Over time, the weight of the world gets shifted onto our shoulders. When we cannot see past our present problems, we need to reset and remember that in the beginning—before the issues at hand, before the obstacles of the day, and before the difficult decisions ahead—God created the heavens and the earth. God is in control. Not us.

God, reset my soul and grant me strength to put my trust in you. You have been the author of creation since the beginning. May I find rest in that reality.

TRAINED EARS

Eli told Samuel, "Go and lie down, and if he calls you, say, 'Speak, Lord, for your servant is listening.'" So, Samuel went and lay down in his place.

1 SAMUEL 3:9 NIV

When listening to music, a musician with a trained ear hears more than the average person. The everyday listener will simply hear a song, but a musician will hear the musical texture, the rhythm, and the key. A trained ear will be able to pick up more and understand the fullness of music. Eli recognized that God was speaking to Samuel, but Samuel did not have a trained ear yet. Instead of explaining what the Lord was doing, Eli taught Samuel how to listen and how to respond. Taking Eli's advice, Samuel went back to bed and was able to hear the voice of the Lord.

As we disciple people in our lives, it may be easier to tell them what to believe. It may be simpler to tell them what God requires, rather than train them how to listen for the voice of the Lord. But we do a disservice to people and stunt their spiritual growth if we don't train their ears to hear God's voice. We need to trust that God desires to teach his children and help them develop the ears to hear the fullness of his music.

God, give me peace as I disciple those around me. Give me ears to hear your voice and the patience to trust your process.

STRENGTH

The LORD is my shepherd;
I have all that I need.
PSALM 23:1 NLT

We see billboards along the highway, advertisements in the paper, and banners on our screens all attempting to pull us into our next purchase. The world has a way of convincing us that something is missing from our lives. Many subscribe to a pattern of thinking that says, If I just get this, then I'll have all I need.

Having new things is not the issue. Purchasing new toys is not the problem. The heart of the matter is wrapped up in believing that our fulfillment comes from what we have, not who we follow. The issue is that we shop for satisfaction, when our shepherd is all we need. Our strength is found in the simplicity of our needs. All we need is the Lord. Anything else is extra. We don't need to scramble for more. We don't have to buy the next best thing. Our shepherd is sufficient. In him, we have all we need.

God, simplify my desires. When my heart desires more things, help me desire more of you. When my mind believes that I am lacking, remind me that you are all I need.

GUIDANCE

*Your word is a lamp to my feet
and a light to my path.*
PSALM 119:105 ESV

As we walk through life, we find ways to increase the distance we can go. We run far and fast as we achieve our way to the next best opportunity. The question, "What's next?" directs our path. The question, "Now what?" dictates our speed. We desire more and let life's opportunities guide our steps. If we invite God into the conversation, we ask for a two-year forecast or a five-year plan. We want him to reveal a clear and accurate picture of the life ahead of us, so we can decide whether we want to take that path. But when we go to God for guidance, we need to understand that speed and distance are not his priority.

We want headlights, but God's Word is a lamp. A lamp can only light up the next few steps of a journey. If we look ahead too far, if we move our feet too fast, we may forget who we're walking with. When God guides our steps and we go at the pace he reveals, we will be going the right direction, toward him. And we will be going the right way, with him.

God, as you light the next steps of my journey, give me the courage to walk in your ways. Guide me closer to you as I lean into the plans you have for my life.

TRUST IN THE LORD

Trust in the LORD with all your heart,
and do not lean on your own understanding.
In all your ways acknowledge him,
and he will make straight your paths.
PROVERBS 3:5-6 ESV

We experience life differently when we trust in the Lord with half our heart and lean hard on our own understanding. The biggest difference is our level of anxiety. When we get swept up in the conflict and confusion of the day, our paths get crisscrossed and we lose our way. We acknowledge the Lord in some of our ways and work hard to pull ourselves out of the mess.

Peace and confidence are byproducts of trusting the Lord. Yet we believe that we'll get there through our own efforts. Life gets the best of us when we continue down the path of self-reliance. But God's grace steps in when we take ourselves out of the equation. When we place our trust in the Lord and acknowledge him in all our ways, peace and confidence will find their way into our hearts and minds.

Lord, give me opportunities to breathe deep today. May I breathe in your presence and exhale my control. I stand before you with open hands and an open heart. Take what is yours and leave peace in my soul.

USE MY WORDS

The tongue can bring death or life;
those who love to talk will reap the consequences.
PROVERBS 18:21 NLT

What we say matters. When we say it matters. How we say it matters. Sticks and stones can certainly break bones, but words can crush a spirit. We underestimate the power of our words, and can undermine our motives if we do not consider the art of conversation. When we pay mind to what we say, we can heal the hurting, restore the weary, and create community. But a loose lip can lead to division and destruction.

After you squeeze toothpaste out of its tube, trying to put it back in is a mess. So, too, are our words. We can try to move forward, but our words are out there. We can try to clean up the mess, but we can't take back what was said. When we understand that our words have the power to bring life or death, we are responsible for using them well. The words people use reflect the words they hear. If we use our words wisely, we can help those around us to understand the power of their words. When we speak words of affirmation to others, we set a good example of how to use words well.

God, help me be quick to listen and slow to speak. Help me use my words wisely to affirm and build others up. Speak life into me and guide my conversations today.

SURRENDER

You can make many plans,
but the LORD's purpose will prevail.
PROVERBS 19:21 NLT

Planning helps us prepare for the unknown. It provides a sense of stability as we journey through life. It has been said, "If you fail to plan, you plan to fail." But sometimes we need to put our plans in perspective. How many things in our lives have turned out the way we planned? What should that teach us? Our plans may fail, but that doesn't mean we're lost. Our plans may be fulfilled, but that doesn't mean we're found. We find ourselves not in the fulfillment of our plans, but in the fulfillment of the Lord's purpose.

The most difficult part of planning is surrendering our plans to him and his purpose. It is a good thing to plan, but when we bind ourselves to our plans, we run the risk of losing hope. When we get married to our plans, we set ourselves up for disappointment. But when we plan with open hands and pursue our plans with the freedom to fail, we can embrace the Lord's purpose with joy, even if we're taken off the path we created for ourselves.

God, as I journey through life in pursuit of you, remind me that your purpose will prevail. Loosen my grip on the plans I have for my life. Open my hands and my heart to joyfully receive the purpose you have for me.

BE MY LIGHT

Do not gloat over me, my enemies!
For though I fall, I will rise again.
Though I sit in darkness, the LORD will be my light.
MICAH 7:8 NLT

Our strength is not measured by how many times we fail. It is not calculated by the number of mistakes we make or the amount of losses we accumulate. The true measure of our strength is found in our source. If we subscribe to the system of self-reliance, the ceiling of our strength is our greatest effort. But if we put our hope in the Lord and find our strength in him, we can rise from our failures and be fearless when darkness descends.

We can fail with confidence when the Lord is the source of our strength. We can sit in the darkness, knowing that the light of the Lord shines brightest in dark times. We do not have to rush out of life's struggles when we know God's strength sustains us in the shadows. The day will come when we realize that our own efforts are not enough. But the sooner we come to that realization, the sooner we can rest in the power of God and be led by the light of the Lord.

God, be my strength. Lord, be my light. Keep my eyes on you when failure finds its way to me. May your light lead me when the shadows of life surround me.

NO LONGER ANXIOUS

"I tell you, do not be anxious about your life, what you will eat or what you will drink, nor about your body, what you will put on. Is not life more than food, and the body more than clothing? Look at the birds of the air: they neither sow nor reap nor gather into barns, and yet your heavenly Father feeds them. Are you not of more value than they?"

MATTHEW 6:25-26 ESV

Many minor things in life consume our care. We find things to worry about and often perceive little things as big problems. But if we take the time to understand the real issue at hand and whose hand we hold as we journey, we will experience a peace that settles our souls.

The issue at hand might be significant in our eyes but already taken care of in God's eyes. Part of the problem is that we confuse our wants with our needs. We get locked into our own desires, and anxiety arises when we are left in want. But Jesus reminds us that our heavenly Father values us more than the birds of the air. He reminds us that our needs have been provided for. If we can rest in that reality, our anxiety will fade away and peace will be present.

God, may your provision bring me peace so I can pay mind to the significant struggles that surround me. Give me perspective and increase my trust in you.

LOVE

Love is patient, love is kind. It does not envy,
it does not boast, it is not proud.
It does not dishonor others, it is not self-seeking,
it is not easily angered, it keeps no record of wrongs.
Love does not delight in evil but rejoices with the truth.
It always protects, always trusts, always hopes,
always perseveres.

1 CORINTHIANS 13:4-7 NIV

Happy Valentine's Day! These verses are often shared at weddings, which is great, but the apostle Paul never mentioned a wedding. That's not to say that these verses can't be applied to marriage; they certainly can be. But the application is so much richer and deeper than just that.

Some people recommend taking out the word love in the verses and inserting our own name. If we do, we'll soon realize that we're really not those things 100 percent, but Jesus is. So the idea is to continue to rely on Jesus, not ourselves. We might do okay for a while, but before long we'll drop the ball. We want to be patient and slow to anger with the people in our lives, but it's really hard sometimes. Don't shame yourself into thinking that if you fail at love, you have somehow upset God. It just shows us how much more we need God.

God, show me your love today. Grow me in my imperfect love and develop me more into the likeness of Christ.

COMPASSION

When he saw the crowds, he had compassion for them,
because they were harassed and helpless,
like sheep without a shepherd.
MATTHEW 9:36 ESV

Compassion for another grows when we understand their story. It unites the mind and the heart. We may see the circumstances surrounding a situation, but when we understand the context, our heart gets involved and compassion springs forth. Compassion means to "suffer with." When we have compassion for someone, their problems become our problems. Their pain becomes our pain. Jesus saw the crowds, and he also knew their situation. Compassion was his natural reaction. When he saw the harassed and helpless people, he had compassion at first sight. Their circumstances did not change in that moment, but their story did. Jesus entered their struggle in that moment, making their problem his own.

We are called to be people of compassion, not judgment. If we take time to understand the stories of those we serve, compassion will be close by. If we learn to have compassion at first sight, we will begin to see beyond ourselves. If we seek to extend grace to those in need, compassion will become a natural part of our lives.

God, lead me into a life of compassion. Give me eyes to see the needs of those around me. Disrupt my comfort and give me the courage to respond with compassion.

LIFE WITH CHRIST

*"Simply join your life with mine. Learn my ways and you'll
discover that I'm gentle, humble, easy to please.
You will find refreshment and rest in me."*
MATTHEW 11:29 TPT

The busyness of life often brings us to our knees. We work hard, play hard, crash hard, and then pray hard. When we run out of gas, we run to our source. We pray for rest and hope to be refueled so we can get back out there. Jesus meets us in our exhaustion, in our brokenness, in our struggles. But he also calls us to a new way of working and reveals a new road to resting. A yoke is a wooden frame that holds two oxen together so they can work side by side. As the stronger ox moves, the weaker ox is pulled along. When both oxen are strong, the workload is lighter for both. This is the picture of work that Jesus paints for us.

Life alone is exhausting. But when we are yoked with Jesus, he is not a pit stop. He's a presence. When we are working by his side, we can rest while we labor, knowing his strength is sufficient. Life with Christ by our side takes us further faster. When we are yoked with Christ, his humbleness rubs off on us, and rest for our souls is always one step away.

God, teach me to walk in your ways. May I experience rest as you draw me into your presence.

COURAGE

Jesus immediately said to them: "Take courage! It is I. Don't be afraid." "Lord, if it's you," Peter replied, "tell me to come to you on the water." "Come," he said. Then Peter got down out of the boat, walked on the water and came toward Jesus.

MATTHEW 14:27-29 NIV

When we are committed to comfort, it's difficult to experience all that God has in store for us. Whether because of the fear of failure or the fear of the unknown, we choose to stay in the boat when we let our fears dictate our direction. Courage is not the absence of fear but the presence of peace when fear is at hand. When our object of hope is greater than our object of fear, we can be courageous.

In the midst of their fear, Jesus said to his disciples, "Take courage! It is I. Don't be afraid." In other words, "Be courageous because I am here. And I am greater than your biggest fear." We can experience peace when we put Jesus on the proper pedestal. When our courage comes from Christ, we will be able to do the unimaginable. We will be able to step out of the boat into the unknown with confidence and accept his simple invitation to come.

God, give me peace when fear surrounds me. Help me to be courageous and follow you into the unknown. Build my trust so I can experience all that you have in store for me.

CREATIVITY

"It will be like a man going on a journey, who called his servants and entrusted to them his property. To one he gave five talents, to another two, to another one, to each according to his ability. Then he went away."

MATTHEW 25:14-15 ESV

One of the first things we do when we get something new is look for instructions. We open the package and find the directions. Instructions are helpful, and it is wise to follow the directions. But what do we do when life gives us something without any instructions? How do we fare when we get an opportunity to use our creativity? In Jesus' time, it would take a servant nearly twenty years to earn one talent. So the servant who received five talents of his master's property had a heavy responsibility to handle. The servants were given a lot to work with, but the master left them without any instructions. Each servant had an opportunity to exercise his creativity and make his master proud.

By the grace of God, we have received gifts and talents to be used for his glory. God guides us, but he leaves us without any specific instructions. Instead, he gives us opportunities to use our creativity and come up with ways to make him proud of his investment in us.

God, awaken my creativity. Inspire my imagination. And help me to be a good and faithful steward of the gifts and talents you have bestowed upon me.

PREPARATION

A voice came from heaven: "You are my Son, whom I love;
with you I am well pleased." At once the Spirit sent him out
into the wilderness.
MARK 1:11-12 NIV

There are seasons in life that are confusing and puzzling.
The circumstances that surround us can make us question
God's motives and even doubt God's love for us. When we
find ourselves in seasons of wilderness, it's important to have
the right posture. We need to have a posture of receiving,
a commitment to growing, and a focus on the future. As
Jesus was being baptized, God affirmed him, saying, "You
are my Son, whom I love; with you I am well pleased." The
puzzling part of the story is that immediately following Jesus'
affirmation, the Spirit led him into the wilderness. When he
was with the wild animals, Jesus didn't question what God
said in the waters. Equipped with God's love, he battled in the
wilderness for forty days.

Sometimes our sin leads us into the wilderness, but other
times God leads us there. Seasons of wilderness reveal and
shape our foundation. We don't have to question his love
when we find ourselves in the struggle. We need to remain in
his love, trust in the process, and let the season of wilderness
prepare us to do powerful things.

God, keep my eyes on you when I find myself in the
wilderness. Shape me in the shadows, and prepare me for
the path ahead.

COMMITMENT

When they could not get near him because of the crowd, they removed the roof above him, and when they had made an opening, they let down the bed on which the paralytic lay. And when Jesus saw their faith, he said to the paralytic, "Son, your sins are forgiven."

MARK 2:4-5 ESV

When obstacles arise or roadblocks impede our path, our commitment to the task at hand is tested. How we handle the hurdles of life reveals what is important to us. If our commitment to the task is stronger than the object in the way, we will use our creativity to complete the task. But if our commitment is frail and our dedication is faint, we will find comfort in quitting.

A crowd could not stop the paralytic's friends from getting him to the feet of Jesus. A roof could not make them quit. Their faith in Christ and their commitment to their friend were far greater than the obstacles that were in the way. Jesus noticed their faith and honored their commitment. By God's power, the paralyzed man walked. By God's grace, the man's sins were forgiven. A commitment to getting others to the feet of Christ is a commitment worth fighting for. Believing in the power of Jesus will take us past any obstacle and over any hurdle we find in the way.

God, increase my commitment to you. Help me see the opportunities beyond the obstacles. And grant me the fortitude to stay the course when quitting sounds comfortable.

PRESENCE IN STORMS

That day when evening came, he said to his disciples, "Let us go over to the other side." Leaving the crowd behind, they took him along, just as he was, in the boat. There were also other boats with him. A furious squall came up, and the waves broke over the boat, so that it was nearly swamped.

MARK 4:35-37 NIV

In life, we can hope for bright days full of sunshine, but dreary nights and stormy skies are part of the journey. The twists and turns we experience can leave us feeling swamped with struggle. But we find our hope in God's presence during the storms of life. Jesus took his disciples on an evening journey on the lake. There were other boats on the same waters, but when the winds picked up, Christ was in the boat with his disciples. When the waters rose, Christ was there. When the waves began to sink the vessel, Christ was there.

Living a life with Christ means having Jesus with us in the storm. When the sickness comes, he is in our boat. When loss overwhelms us, he is with us. When confusion capsizes us, he is our comforter. During the storm, it is better to be in a boat with Jesus than out on the waters without him.

God, may I find my comfort in you and experience peace through your presence. When the storms of life overwhelm me, be the hope that carries me to the other side.

JUST BELIEVE

While Jesus was still speaking, some people came from the house of Jairus, the synagogue leader. "Your daughter is dead," they said. "Why bother the teacher anymore?" Overhearing what they said, Jesus told him, "Don't be afraid; just believe."
MARK 5:35-36 NIV

When life doesn't go as planned, we often fear the unknown and put our faith in a new plan. We listen to our fears and head toward hopelessness. Our internal doubts are reinforced by a spirit of negativity. We give power to the critics as their words extinguish our hope. But Jesus overhears our distracting internal dialogue and desires to give us a new voice to listen to—a voice that says, "Do not be afraid. Just believe."

As a commander in an army directs the soldiers, Jesus spoke those words to Jairus as a command: an imperative, not a suggestion. Jesus didn't declare it to the crowd; he spoke past his doubters directly to Jairus. As with Jairus, Jesus desires to pull us out of our hopelessness and beyond our fear. He wants us to put our faith in him, not a new plan. His words may not always be louder than the words of his critics, but they are more powerful and come from a higher authority.

God, give me ears to hear your voice when doubt sets in. Restore my faith in you when my plans fail. Move me beyond my fears to a place of belief, hope, and promise.

LIKE A CHILD

"Truly I tell you, anyone who will not receive the kingdom of God like a little child will never enter it."
Mark 10:15 NIV

When we take a new job, we need to go through two things: an application process and a training period to make sure we can carry out the required tasks. So if we believe the kingdom of God is bigger than any job we apply for, we would expect that entrance also requires a strenuous process. But Jesus defies our expectations and explains that receiving the kingdom requires humbleness and humility, not an application and training.

The process to enter the kingdom isn't strenuous, but it isn't easy either. To become "like a little child" means becoming dependent. It means stripping away all that makes us strong and self-reliant, and that goes against "growing up" and becoming independent. But it makes complete sense if we want to be grafted into the kingdom and become dependent on the King. When we are self-reliant, we buy into the lie that we are all we need. But when we commit to humbleness and humility, we realize how much we need God in our lives. If we receive the kingdom like a little child, humbly and dependently, we will be able to accomplish more than we ever could on our own.

God, humble my spirit and make me more reliant on you. Help me become like a little child so I can receive the kingdom with awe and wonder.

SERVANT LEADERSHIP

"Even the Son of Man did not come to be served, but to serve, and to give his life as a ransom for many."
MARK 10:45 NIV

It is the call of our culture to climb the ladder of power and authority. Many people find their life purpose in that pursuit. We prize promotions and are defined by the titles we hold. We use others to get what we want and invest in relationships only if it benefits us to do so. Yet Jesus had a different pathway to power and influence. Christ's path was paved with service and sacrifice. Jesus not only served but was also a servant. His actions came out of his character, out of who he was.

Positions of power and authority are honorable positions to hold. However, the attitude of entitlement that comes with those positions is something we need to let go of. When we take the path of Christ, seeking to serve and sacrifice for the sake of others, we will create a culture that reflects the kingdom.

God, give me the eyes to see the ways I can be a servant today. Give me the courage to step into those opportunities. Help me develop the habit of helping others, so service and sacrifice become a natural rhythm of my life.

GRACE

"'I am no longer worthy to be called your son. Treat me as one of your hired servants.' And he arose and came to his father. But while he was still a long way off, his father saw him and felt compassion, and ran and embraced him and kissed him."
LUKE 15:19-20 ESV

When we make choices that bring us away from the Lord, we convince ourselves that we need to earn our way back. Our poor decisions bring us to a distant land, and we begin to lose our identity as a child of God. If we do not understand the depth of God's grace, we try to direct God in dealing with our disobedience.

In the parable of the prodigal son, the son had a plan and a proposal. The plan was to go home, and the proposal was to become a hired servant of his father. He did not understand the grace of his father and bought into the lie that he had to earn his way back into the fold. But the father had a different plan and a different proposal. His plan was to lovingly welcome his son home, and his proposal was a family celebration. The parable is about the grace of the father, not the efforts of the son. We cannot give to others what we do not have for ourselves. Once we receive God's grace in our own lives, we can extend it to those we love.

God of love, be by my side. God of grace, be my guide.

SACRIFICE

He said to them, "Truly, I say to you, there is no one who has left house or wife or brothers or parents or children, for the sake of the kingdom of God, who will not receive many times more in this time, and in the age to come eternal life."
LUKE 18:29-30 ESV

The weight of sacrifice is not a light load to carry. Sacrifice is a loss that evokes pain, but it also ushers in something new. Jesus doesn't call us to sacrifice for the sake of loss, but for the sake of the kingdom. When we put Christ and the kingdom at the top of our priority list, we'll be able to look beyond the object of sacrifice to what is gained through our loss. The promise is that the benefits will outweigh our sacrifice, not only in this time but also in the age to come.

When we choose to live a sacrificial life, we'll experience life to the full. We'll experience a life with Christ as our supply. And with him as our supply, we have enough life to pour into those around us.

Lord Jesus, help me to focus on you and your kingdom. Give me the strength to surrender all I am and all I have to you. Pour into my life so I can begin to see the joy beyond the sacrifice.

ROUTINES

Jesus said to her, "Everyone who drinks of this water will be thirsty again, but whoever drinks of the water that I will give him will never be thirsty again. The water that I will give him will become in him a spring of water welling up to eternal life."
JOHN 4:13-14 ESV

Our daily routines can condition us into comfortable living. We settle for repeated rhythms and expect our lives to change. Day after day, month after month, year after year, we find life in the things that satisfy only our immediate needs and desires. Our hearts long for so much more, but we settle for so much less.

Too often we live for the temporary, but Christ invites us into the life our souls are longing for. If we allow Jesus to disrupt our daily patterns of living, we can develop the eyes to see the alternative life that Christ offers. A life that satisfies beyond our temporary needs and desires. A life that generates more life. A life that brings light to our work and our play. A life that spills over into our families and our friends.

God, help me encounter you beyond my daily routines. Disrupt my comfort so I will be open to receiving the life that you graciously offer. Mold my heart so I will desire the eternal things you place before me.

THE PRESENCE

The woman said, "I know that Messiah" (called Christ) "is coming. When he comes, he will explain everything to us." Then Jesus declared, "I, the one speaking to you—I am he."
JOHN 4:25-26 NIV

Understanding is not a prerequisite of having faith. It is possible to cling to a promise when we find ourselves in the midst of confusion and doubt. Sometimes we are distracted by our circumstances. Sometimes we are blinded by our own expectations. Sometimes Jesus is standing right in front of us, but we're so consumed by our pursuit of him that we fail to recognize his presence.

The Samaritan woman had an unplanned encounter with a Jewish prophet by Jacob's well. The conversation brought her past to light, uncovered her questions, and revealed her faith in the promise of the coming "Messiah." She didn't know all the details, but she knew one thing for sure: "The Christ is coming to explain everything." When she declared her faith in that promise, Jesus revealed his true identity to her. Life will bring us through valleys of doubt and clouds of confusion. But when we have faith and cling to the promise of the coming Messiah, we may come to find that Christ was with us the entire time.

God, when confusion and doubt overwhelm me, help me put my hope in you. When I am blinded by my circumstances, give me faith to know that you are near.

BEING CONTENT

Not that I was ever in need,
for I have learned how to be content with whatever I have.
PHILIPPIANS 4:11 NLT

It could never be said that Paul had it easy. Maybe you can relate to what he went through. His life was riddled with ups and downs. He faced hardships and successes, agony and abuse, rejection as well as acceptance, and shame but also joy. Paul had made huge mistakes and caused tremendous pain that scarred his past, but his life changed dramatically when he met Jesus. He began to help others and learned to share himself vulnerably. Instead of bullying his way to victory, he would sometimes go hungry. Instead of being celebrated, he would sometimes suffer loss.

Yet, because of Jesus, Paul found contentment. He learned that no matter his circumstances, he was grounded in who he was because of who Jesus was in his life. He found confidence in what he was called to do because of what Jesus was calling him to do. As a man, where do you find contentment? What enables you to stand courageously? What helps you feel secure in who you are and what you're called to do? Hopefully, you will find your inner strength in the life and power of Jesus Christ today.

God, help me find my sense of worth, my sense of peace, and my sense of identity in you. Let me trust you fully for the contentment I so desperately seek in my life.

TRUSTING GOD TO SUPPLY

This same God who takes care of me
will supply all your needs from his glorious riches,
which have been given to us in Christ Jesus.
PHILIPPIANS 4:19 NLT

Consider all the things that have been set before you. What do you have? What do you lack? What raises you to your feet in joy? What brings you to your knees in sadness? Whose steps are crossing your path? What words are ready to come out of your mouth? What passions are ready to well up in your heart? What sights are you absorbing with your eyes? That's quite a list. Whether you have much or whether you have little, your life is full.

Considering all that is set before you, what do you need? God the Father has unlimited resources. Do you have responsibilities set before you? What does God have at his disposal that could help you fulfill your calling? Do you have people in your life who need your love? How could God supply your needs in such a way that you could unconditionally love them? Do you lack strength or courage within yourself today? How might the Lord of all creation want to bless you heart, mind, soul, and strength?

God, let me seek you first and there find my needs supplied in you.

JULY

He gives power to the weak
and strength to the powerless.

ISAIAH 40:29 NLT

THE OFF SWITCH

*"Six days you shall labor and do all your work,
but the seventh day is a sabbath to the LORD your God.
On it you shall not do any work."*
EXODUS 20:9-10 NIV

Have you ever had a machine that was hard to turn off? Maybe there was a specific process of steps and patience needed before it could actually turn off. Maybe a switch was stuck, leaving it in the on position. Maybe something internally was broken, preventing anything from turning it off. Often, this is an unfortunate picture of us. Stuck in the on position, we run until our circuits are fried or our batteries go dead. We tell ourselves that after one more e-mail, we'll be done for the night. We convince ourselves that this phone call is important enough to step away from friends or family just for a bit. We can't turn off.

God gave the Israelites a mandatory off switch. It was called the Sabbath. This off switch was a way they honored God, as they remembered that the world's problems and opportunities didn't rest on their shoulders. But it didn't only honor God; it was also good for them. They, unlike many of us, had a rhythm of rest and work, and a rest kept them from burning out. This week, consider taking some time to rest. Do something that honors God and fills you up.

God, the world doesn't depend on me. You are in control. I don't need to labor anxiously without rest. Help me to truly believe that this week, and to honor you through rest.

YOUR CROSS

Jesus said to his disciples, "Whoever wants to be my disciple must deny themselves and take up their cross and follow me."
MATTHEW 16:24 NIV

Following Jesus is a path of great joy but also real sacrifice. Often when we hear the word sacrifice, we think of maybe a mission field or giving away a large amount of money. That's all well and good and is sometimes what God is calling us to do.

But more often, sacrifice looks like waking up at 3 a.m. to help out a sick friend, taking time during your evening to volunteer at a local soup kitchen, or praying with a co-worker. These are the little sacrifices that, when practiced through the course of years, reap the greatest rewards. What might be your "cross" today? How can you take it up and, in so doing, follow Jesus?

Father, help me to be ready to sacrifice my time and energy for those closest to me. I desire that I might love like you love. Give me strength to do this.

AFFIRMATION

Jacob took the food to his father. "My father?" he said. "Yes, my son," Isaac answered. "Who are you—Esau or Jacob?"
GENESIS 27:18 NLT

Isaac had always preferred his older son, Esau, to his younger son, Jacob. After all, Esau could hunt and possessed other masculine attributes. Meanwhile, Jacob hung out at home and was also a little conniving while Esau was simpler. Isaac's heart gravitated toward his older boy. Near the end of Isaac's life, Jacob, in a crazy effort to take Esau's inheritance, dressed up like his older brother and deceived his aging father. Jacob was a bit of a sneak, but can you imagine knowing that you're second to your brother when it comes to Dad's love? That's hard to swallow.

Even though this situation is in some ways a little far-fetched, experience reminds us how common it is. Many of us live with an affirmation vacancy, a place where we didn't receive like we desired. The trick is to remember that when we feel the need for love, we need to remember God, who gave his one and only Son so that we might be called his kids. That's a love that can heal affirmation vacancies. That's a love that provides an example of how to let our love spill out to those around us.

Father, teach me your ways. Help me to love like you do! I want to know your love for myself and to pass it on to others.

OUR FATHER

"This, then, is how you should pray:
'Our Father....'"
MATTHEW 6:9 NIV

Throughout the Bible, we find many titles for God. We learn that God is creator and powerful, that he is sovereign and knows all. But in the New Testament, when Jesus is sharing how his followers should pray, he calls him, "Our Father." Let that sink in.

The infinite, sovereign Creator God wants you to know him as "Dad." Not only that, but Jesus speaks about God being the type of father who scans the horizon, looking for lost sons and daughters, and then runs to them when he sees even a hint of them (Luke 19). God is a father, and the Father's love is intimate and protective and yearns to know and be known.

God, you are all-powerful, but you also desire intimacy. You want to be known as Dad. Help me to know you as a kind father today.

HALLOWED BE

"Hallowed be your name."
MATTHEW 6:9 NIV

When most people hear the word holy, they think "moral" or "religious." That's not exactly wrong, but it misses the rich biblical meaning. Holy really means "set apart" or "other." A few theologians have suggested that when we see holy, we should think of "wholly other." God is perfect; we're not. God is all-powerful; we're not. You get the idea. In the Old Testament, priests had to perform certain purity rituals to come near God. Why? Because God is holy and they weren't. To approach God, they had to purify themselves, becoming holy.

It's interesting that Jesus says we should call God "Father" but also know he is holy. Jesus wants us to hold these two important truths together. God is beyond, and God is near. God is powerful, and God is meek. God is a warrior, and God is loving. It's as if Jesus, right at the beginning of the Lord's Prayer, was inviting us into the beautiful mystery of who God is. When you reflect on this, you may start to stagger. It may blow you away. And if it does, you're on the right track.

Oh God, all-powerful and holy God, intimate and loving Father. Help me to be amazed by you. May I draw near to you today.

YOUR WILL BE DONE

"Your kingdom come, your will be done.
On earth as it is in heaven."
MATTHEW 6:10 NIV

In the ancient world, a kingdom was a place where the values and way of life that the king desired were put into practice. As you can imagine, this could be good or bad depending on the king. Jesus is the ultimate good King. Throughout the Gospels (Matthew, Mark, Luke, and John), he heals the sick; includes the social, spiritual, and racial outcasts into his family; and ultimately makes a public spectacle of the world's power by triumphing over it through death. The kingdom of Jesus is like no other.

As we align ourselves with this God who is both beyond and near, we must take up the cause of his kingdom. This can be hard. Within each of us is a little ruler that, left alone, would set up a kingdom that runs according to our basic desires and wants. As we learn to pray like Jesus, we must lay down our kingdoms and take up his kingdom mission. This doesn't mean that everyone becomes a pastor. It doesn't mean that we have to live at the church. It does mean that we, like Jesus, should have a heart for the outcast and vulnerable. It does mean we should familiarize ourselves with sacrifice. And it does mean that we should make Jesus our first allegiance—in all areas of life.

God, give me strength to live for your kingdom. Give me your power to love my family, my coworkers, and my neighbors. Help me to desire your kingdom!

DAILY BREAD

"Give us today our daily bread."
MATTHEW 6:11 NIV

God is not concerned only with your spiritual needs. He is interested and desires to be recognized in and through all things; after all, he is the one who made it all. Yep, that even means the food you eat.

Previous generations had a much more intimate relationship with their food. They often raised and slaughtered the meat they ate. They depended on the rain and the sun to be "enough." While we can just pick up a loaf of bread, previous generations saw the wheat grow from the soil. So the prayer below might make more intuitive sense to a group of Jews or Christians from a few centuries ago. Still, when we pray for our "daily bread," we recognize that God is God of every square inch of creation. We remember that he made it all and cares for all of us. And we then remember that everything, even a slice of toast in the morning, is a gift of grace.

God, thank you for the easily forgotten gifts: for food and friendship, family and employment. You are generous, and I thank you for being my provider.

FORGIVE AS

*"Forgive us our debts,
as we have also forgiven our debtors."*
MATTHEW 6:12 NIV

Forgiveness is one of those words that sounds beautiful but is terribly hard to put into practice. Perhaps that's the best description of it: a beautiful difficulty. Forgiveness shows up as a beautiful difficulty when a grown woman finds the strength to forgive a mean stepfather and finds the freedom that forgiveness always brings. A beautiful difficulty takes place when a husband says, "I love you, and I forgive you," to his wife who has just admitted to a moral struggle. This beautiful difficulty shows up when a business owner hugs an employee who has just been caught cutting corners.

However, the best picture of forgiveness as a beautiful difficulty is the cross. On the cross Jesus bore the difficult weight of our sin and offered the beautiful gift of divine forgiveness. When we understand that beautiful difficulty, our calls to forgiveness become a bit less difficult.

Oh God, thank you for your forgiveness. Thank you for the cross. Help me to remember that you forgave me, all of me, and I will remember to forgive those who have hurt or offended me.

LEAD US NOT

"Lead us not into temptation,
but deliver us from the evil one."
MATTHEW 6:13 NIV

Jesus' prayer concludes with a request to not be led into temptation. Sometimes when we're struggling to overcome a temptation, we find ourselves more likely than ever to start focusing on it. The second a temptation is mentioned is the moment we can't get it out of our head. Just say the words ice cream to someone who's counting calories and you'll know what I mean. The solution to overcoming temptation is to focus on something better than what is tempting us.

There's a reason why Scripture speaks multiple times of fixing our eyes on Jesus. When our eyes are fixed on him, temptations become "strangely dim." Why? Because our gaze is on something far better than the diversions our culture throws at us. Indeed, our gaze is on the one whom our hearts truly crave.

God, you are worthy of my complete focus. Help me to see you in your power and strength today. May I get a glimpse of you in your love. Then I will not slip into distractions.

BE ONE

*"That all of them may be one, Father,
just as you are in me and I am in you."*
JOHN 17:21 NIV

A team will rise and fall based on how unified it is. It doesn't matter if it's a company, a platoon, a soccer team, or a family. Relational fracture in a team environment leads to failure. The 2004 United States Olympic basketball team is one example. Although they were the best players in the world, they fell short of gold. This happened because each person wanted to be the star; they weren't unified. A team's fracture leads to a team's failure. It's that simple.

Simple, sure, but hard to put into practice. The second you have any type of team, you have broken and rebellious human beings in the same environment, and there's bound to be tension. Like porcupines cuddling in the cold, we often hurt each other as we seek connection. But just as often as there is fracture, there is also the opposite—harmony. When two voices harmonize, a beautiful song can result. The same is true when lives merge in a team environment. This is why Jesus prays that his disciples (throughout all ages of the church) might be "one." Jesus wants harmony, not fracture.

God, today I pray for all the relationships in my life. I pray that I would be, through your work, a harmonizing voice, a team player, and a loving friend. Help me with this, God, because by myself, I slip up and make it about me.

PROOF

"May they also be in us so that the world
may believe that you have sent me."
JOHN 17:21 NIV

The proof is in the pudding the old adage says, meaning the only thing that really matters is if something works. You get it, right? In the end, the advertising and sale price mean nothing if the product falls apart right when you open it.

Jesus continues to pray for unity, suggesting that when the church is unified, the world will believe. The proof of the church is in the unity here, we might say. That means that when it comes to unity, there is something on the line: our spiritual integrity and our testimony to a world that needs to know God's love.

God, help me to radiate your love so the world will know your love. May I live a life of unity so the world will know your power and love!

OUR HELPER

"I have given them the glory that you gave me,
that they may be one as we are one."
JOHN 17:22 NIV

Have you ever been asked to do something, maybe a particular job at work or an essay in a class, without the proper resources or training to accomplish the goal? If so, what was the result? More often than not, it's suboptimal. When it comes to Christian unity, Jesus has thankfully not left us under resourced! In the above verse, Jesus describes Christian unity as a reachable goal. Not because we're really talented or incredibly friendly. Nope. From Jesus' perspective, Christian unity is possible because he's given us his glory, which is God's very presence in the life of his believers. The presence of God in the followers of Christ brings real and lasting Christian unity.

In a way, this is encouraging. Jesus hasn't left us to figure it out. He's given us a helper, his Holy Spirit. But, in another way, this means we have to work at it. Unity doesn't come naturally; we have to yield to others and the Holy Spirit. We have to lay down our agendas. If we really want the unity that Christ has prayed we would experience, we have to keep in step with the Spirit, saying daily, "Not my will, but yours."

God, I confess I need you. Specifically, I need your Holy Spirit in my life. I want to see you work. I want to grow as a man. For that I need your presence. Please give me your strength today.

ONE BODY

In Christ we, though many, form one body,
and each member belongs to all the others.
ROMANS 12:5 NIV

A bicycle has many parts. The handlebars help us turn corners or keep the bike straight while cruising downhill. The gears can shift with a touch of the fingers, helping us climb hills. The pedals that connect to the gears move the chain and the rear wheel. And the brakes let us stop when the light turns red. If we took one of these parts away, the bike wouldn't work or would be dangerous to ride.

Now think of your family, your church, or even your workplace. There are those who are gifted with administration; they can organize and create systems. There are gregarious extroverts, always making new connections. Some have a kind and warm presence, the type that make you feel safe. Cautious and conservative personalities help us play it safe and not wade recklessly into new waters. Pioneers balance the cautious voices and challenge us to have faith and get out of the boat even when it's uncomfortable. Creative types imagine beautiful God-honoring creations that inspire us to be in awe of God. Then there are the straight shooters who can look you in the eye and tell you what you need to hear. If you took away one type of person from your family, church, or workplace, the difference would be noticeable.

God, help me to recognize and honor the diversity you have placed in my home, church, and workplace.

LEGACY

*"My prayer is not for them alone.
I pray also for those who will believe in me
through their message."*
JOHN 17:20 NIV

What do you think of when you hear the word legacy? Do you think about money? Or some family values passed down through generations? Jesus prayed the ultimate "legacy" prayer as the cross got closer. In that prayer he didn't just pray for himself, though he was in the midst of crisis. He didn't even pray just for his friends and followers, though they would soon face crisis. Toward the end of Jesus' earthly life, he prayed for us. That is amazing. You. Me. The person in your small group who always shows up late. Everyone. Jesus, in one of his last moments on earth, thought about us.

What would it look like for you to think two or three generations beyond you? How might that affect your life? When you think about that, you start getting a vision for leaving a legacy, and you're closer to having the mind of Christ (1 Corinthians 2:16).

God, give me a vision for my life that is bigger than me. I pray for a vision for my future that is even bigger than I can imagine; a God-sized vision. Help me to think about the legacy I am passing down. I desire it to be one that honors you. Please give me strength.

SET ON

Blessed are those whose strength is in you,
whose hearts are set on pilgrimage.
PSALM 84:5 NIV

What is your heart set on? One way to tell is to think about what you spend your time thinking about. Another could be to consider where you spend your money or time. The psalmist says that the blessed have set their hearts on a journey. The word pilgrimage means a pursuit after something that has real meaning—something that is spiritually significant. So it's bigger than the next raise or a new house.

The man who has set his heart on pilgrimage is pursuing something that is bigger than himself. The man who has set his heart on pilgrimage knows his weaknesses and moral deficiencies and is seeking to grow in those areas. The man who has set his heart on pilgrimage is pursuing Jesus. It is that man who is truly blessed.

Father, I want my heart focus to be on you. I don't want to settle for lesser things or smaller goals. I want your plans to be my plans. So I surrender. You will be my life journey's destination.

HEARTBROKEN

"When I heard these things, I sat down and wept.
For some days I mourned and fasted
and prayed before the God of heaven."
NEHEMIAH 1:4 NIV

Have you ever experienced something in your life that upset you deeply? Typically, we see these experiences as negative, and they often are. But they also have the power to propel us toward action. A quick survey of history shows that the men who have affected the world most positively have been moved to action by some grave need, something that broke their heart. Nehemiah is one example. When he heard about the destruction of his hometown, his heart broke and that led him to return to his hometown and work for its restoration. He surveyed the problem and got an understanding of what needed to be done. He gathered people to help restore the broken walls and structures. He persevered through challenges when people mocked his efforts. All of this happened because his heart broke when he heard some news.

So what gets close to breaking your heart right now? Is it a family you know that is in need? Is it neighborhood kids who need a good male influence? Is it for people to know the loving kindness of God? When you're able to answer those questions, you may, like Nehemiah, be sent into action.

Father, help me to have a heart that breaks for the things that break your heart. Help me then know what to do.

OPPOSITION

Tobiah the Ammonite, who was at his side, said, "What they are building—even a fox climbing up on it would break down their wall of stones!"

NEHEMIAH 4:3 NIV

What do you do in the face of opposition? It's easy to let opposition push us into a sense of defeat. Other times it's easy to lash out, launching a counterattack at the person who opposes us. Perhaps hardest of all is to persevere, pressing through the opposition. You may remember that Nehemiah's heart had broken when he heard the news of his hometown lying in ruins. He went home and sought its restoration. But not too long into that process, he met opposition. He didn't spout back insults or sink into defeat. Instead he found strength to persevere. His secret to this is found in prayer: the first thing he did when the critics raised their voices.

When you're seeking to make a positive impact, you will encounter opposition. The opposition comes internally as you experience self-doubt and find yourself distracted. The opposition comes externally as you hear the voices of critics and questioners. Whether the opposition is internal or external, the path of perseverance begins with prayer. It's when we pray that we are reminded by God of the urgency of what we're doing and find the strength to keep at it.

God, help me to persevere. Remind me of the urgency of caring for those around me. Remind me of the importance of showing your love in my neighborhood. Remind me of how the stakes are high.

CHRIST IN ME

I have been crucified with Christ and I no longer live, but Christ lives in me. The life I now live in the body, I live by faith in the Son of God, who loved me and gave himself for me.
GALATIANS 2:20 NIV

How does it feel when you can't find your wallet? You may lose sleep or be late for work as you look under every couch cushion. If you have to drive somewhere, no doubt you feel a little jittery. Your wallet says something about who you are. In a way, it holds your identity. But the question of identity is bigger than what's in your wallet. "Who am I?" is a question we ask in a variety of ways, and often these identity questions manifest around the topic of achievement. Many of us define ourselves by what we have done or what we weren't able to do. Deriving identity from achievement often sends us into crisis as we realize our limitations and weaknesses.

Paul gives us a different way to derive our identity. In the above passage, he says that the very core of who we are is connected with Jesus Christ. He provides our identity. And because of that, we are accepted despite our achievements (or lack of them). We are given an identity that cannot be lost because of Christ's achievement on our behalf.

Father, remind me that I am in Christ. Help me to remember that, in the end, that is what defines me. Give me the clarity of mind to remember that he is ultimately my identity.

STATUS SYMBOL

Here is neither Jew nor Gentile, neither slave nor free, nor is there male and female, for you are all one in Christ Jesus.
GALATIANS 3:28 NIV

One of the first questions we tend to ask someone we just meet is, "What is it that you do?" By "do," we mean what they do for work. The answer to the question, whether we admit it or not, determines what we think of them. If they reply, "I'm a doctor," our respect quotient goes up and we may even feel a bit insecure. It's easy for this harmless question to slip into a search for status. When someone has more education or a better job, we become insecure about our status. If someone has a wider network, we're left wondering about our status.

Paul, writing to the Galatians, dismantles the major status symbols and positions of his day. For him, a slave is on the same level as a free person. A Jew is on the same level as a Gentile. A woman is on the same level as a man. No one is above and no one is below. This is the case because before Christ we all were in a desperate situation, and in Christ we have been given more than we could ask or imagine. For Paul, the ultimate status symbol is not a new car or a great job, but the cross.

God, help me to believe that the only thing I need for significance is you. Keep me from insecurity and pride. Remind me of who I am in you.

FREEDOM

It is for freedom that Christ has set us free. Stand firm, then, and do not let yourselves be burdened again by a yoke of slavery. You, my brothers and sisters, were called to be free. But do not use your freedom to indulge the flesh; rather, serve one another humbly in love.

GALATIANS 5:1, 13 NIV

It probably wouldn't take you long to think of a movie or book where the plot is all about the pursuit of freedom. We love stories of people being freed from captivity or oppressive situations. For Americans it's woven into our cultural DNA with phrases like "home of the free" and others like it. Interestingly, the Bible is on the same page. Paul challenged the Galatians because they made their faith all about rule adherence. Paul wanted them to know that true faith means freedom from a religion strictly focused on rules and regulations.

Culturally, we love the idea of being freed from others' approval, rule-based religion, or self-criticism, and understandably so. But there is more to freedom than escaping something. In Galatians 5:1, Paul speaks about being freed from the law, but then in verse 13 he says that we have been freed for a purpose. True freedom means that we have been freed from the religious rules and regulations through Christ's work on the cross and that we are freed for the purpose of loving God and the world. Both are essential elements of true freedom.

Father, remind me that I am free from the law. Remind me that I am freed for a purpose—to love.

INVITATION

After this I saw a vast crowd, too great to count, from every nation and tribe and people and language, standing in front of the throne and before the Lamb.

REVELATION 7:9 NIV

Whether it's a holiday celebration or a dinner party for family or friends from work, one of the important questions for all gatherings is, "How many people should we invite?" It may not be a popular or easy decision, but in the end, certain people are on the guest list and others aren't. This process can cause anxiety on the part of those extending the invitations and sometimes cause frustration for those not invited. Still, it's all part of the process.

When John, the author of Revelation, got a glimpse of heaven, he saw people from all continents, people groups, and economic backgrounds right next to each other. Jesus' invitation to his never-ending party isn't limited; it's open to all. Everyone is invited. While our earthly party invitations have understandable limits, what would it look like for us to live knowing that all have been invited to the heavenly banquet?

God, help me to include, not exclude. Help me to welcome, not shun. And help me to still love those who may exclude me. For all this I need your strength.

EVANGELISM

*Pray for us, too, that God will give us many opportunities
to speak about his mysterious plan concerning Christ.
That is why I am here in chains.*
COLOSSIANS 4:3 NLT

Evangelism is one word that those inside and outside
the church dislike equally. It can bring anxiety as some feel
obligated, but not equipped, or nervous about what the
person they're talking to might say. Others feel they're being
pushy and worry about coming off as rude or "more holy
than." Some of this anxiety exists because we haven't always
had great examples. It's easy to think of the guy on the
sidewalk shouting cringe-worthy comments. In contrast to that
caricature, Paul asks the Colossian church to pray that God
would open doors. Paul's method of evangelism was praying
for open doors, not barging through them.

That isn't to excuse us from doing the work of evangelism.
Everyone who has heard the good news of the gospel is called
to pass it on. And every day there are open doors. Evangelism
requires patience and watchful prayer. It involves being in
relationship with those who don't know Christ. It takes being in
a friendship long enough to see God crack open the door of
a person's heart. It means saying something simple like, "You
know, I've been wondering, how can I pray for you?"

God, give me eyes to see the open doors for your gospel!

QUALIFYING

"Go. I am sending you to Pharaoh to bring my people the Israelites out of Egypt." But Moses said to God, "Who am I that I should go to Pharaoh and bring the Israelites out of Egypt?"

Exodus 3:10-11

Have you ever felt ill-equipped to perform a duty? Perhaps you experienced it during a tense conversation with a family member. Maybe it was your first day at a new position. Or perhaps it was while walking out of the hospital after the death of a parent. Whether you're experiencing it now or see it coming in the future, the question, "Am I really up to the task?" is one that haunts many men. It was the fear that plagued Moses' mind as God called him to lead the Israelites to freedom. And, in a way, Moses' concern wasn't unfounded. He wasn't completely up to the task. He apparently stuttered (Exodus 4:10), he had skipped town after killing someone in an angry outburst (Exodus 2:12), and his resume didn't fit the role. But God doesn't call the qualified; he qualifies the called.

Take some time to survey your life. Where do you have an inkling of insecurity? Is it in a particular friendship? Or possibly at work? Wherever it is, know that God is there with you, and as you seek him out, he will guide your steps.

God, I confess I doubt your ability to use me. Help me to trust you. Help me to believe that you want to use me.

CHALLENGE AND GROWTH

These have come so that the proven genuineness of your faith—of greater worth than gold, which perishes even though refined by fire—may result in praise, glory and honor when Jesus Christ is revealed.

1 PETER 1:7 NIV

Lift weights and you'll find yourself sore. Decide to run a 10K race and you'll have to push through pain. Work on strained relationship and you'll have to have tough conversations about those easily overlooked growth areas. Buy a house and you'll have to be disciplined and ruthless in saving for a down payment. As much as we'd like to have maturity come easy, it seems that challenge and growth are inseparable.

The people Peter was writing to (exiles scattered throughout the provinces of Pontus, Galatia, Cappadocia, Asia, and Bithynia) didn't have much money, and their neighbors and coworkers were slandering them for their faith. Even more, these exiles most likely didn't have social status and therefore had no real opportunities for advancement. All of that together created a challenging situation. But Peter says that what they did have in one another and in Christ was of greater worth than gold. Not only that, but this hidden wealth became more pure and strong in opposition. Again we find that challenge and growth are inseparable.

God, help me to welcome challenges. Give me eyes to see what you're doing in me in times of difficulty. Give me faith to believe that what I have in you is of greater worth than gold.

DESIRING GOD

Though you have not seen him, you love him; and even though you do not see him now, you believe in him and are filled with an inexpressible and glorious joy.
1 PETER 1:8 NIV

As kids head off to college, parents often find themselves gazing at family photos that capture moments of times long gone by. Others may pull out their phone and scroll through a couple of pictures of loved ones when away from home. Absence makes the heart grow fonder, the old adage goes. The recipients of Peter's first letter never had the chance to meet Jesus face-to-face, but when they heard about him through the missionary efforts of the early church, something changed in them. They found themselves loving Jesus and being filled with joy as they anticipated an eternity with him.

But just as absence can make a heart grow fonder, it also can produce forgetfulness. The recipients of Peter's letter experienced a growth of desire for the Lord, not forgetfulness. Why? Because as parents do with pictures of their family, they held the reality of Jesus before them as often as possible, and this gave them great joy.

Father, I have not seen you; help me to love you. I desire to know you; help me to desire you more.

GET AWAY

Very early in the morning, while it was still dark, Jesus got up, left the house and went off to a solitary place, where he prayed. Simon and his companions went to look for him, and when they found him, they exclaimed: "Everyone is looking for you!"

MARK 1:35-37 NIV

Jesus was not worried about the crowd. Sure, he loved them. But Jesus' primary concern was connection with his Father. He knew that connection was where strength came from. Any healing and hope for the crowds rested on his intermingling with the Spirit and the Father. But Simon (or Peter) was worried. The crowd was looking for Jesus, and if Jesus didn't show up soon, they might disappear. Then what would happen to the movement? Didn't Jesus understand that Simon had invested his life in this movement? If the crowd left, what would happen to his investment? He'd have to sulk back and buy his fishing gear back. *Sigh.*

Why did Jesus not give in to Peter's anxiety? Jesus knew that the popularity of the crowd didn't define him. He knew that his priority wasn't the court of public approval or even seeing his movement go up in the rankings. He knew that his Father's voice and the Spirit's presence are the most important, and that the identity they offer will not be taken away.

God, give me the courage to get away today. I don't have to endlessly win favor from the crowds. What I need is to hear the voice of your favor.

THE CALLING OF WORK

The Lord God took the man and put him in the Garden of Eden to work it and take care of it.
GENESIS 2:15 NIV

"I'm working for the weekend," we sometimes say. It's understandable. Often our sights are set on that weekend getaway or just some relaxing time with the family. Even more, work environments can be stressful and further stir up a 5 p.m. anticipation. Early in the book of Genesis we see God's stamp of approval on work. This may be contrary to what we've thought about the garden of Eden. Wouldn't "paradise" involve sun umbrellas and tropical drinks? Maybe, but it also involved work. Because we were made in the image of God, and God worked by creating the world, we too have within us a compulsion to create and make—to work.

What if God placed you in your workplace just as he placed Adam in the garden? What would it look like to honor him there? What would it look like to find joy in the process of work? How could you respond to God's invitation to love both him and people right there, at work?

God, help me to find joy while I work. I want it to be more than a grind. I want my attitude at work to honor you. Help me to take pride in what I do.

HIDING

The man and his wife heard the sound of the LORD God as he was walking in the garden in the cool of the day, and they hid from the LORD God among the trees of the garden.

GENESIS 3:8 NIV

We don't stop playing hide-and-go-seek when we're young. We keep playing far into adulthood, though the stakes change and it's no longer fun. When someone we have an unresolved disagreement with walks into a store, we jet down a grocery aisle out of sight. When our boss asks how the "big project" is coming, we look down. Since we don't want our friends or family to know how much we drink, we keep our beer or liquor in the garage.

Why do we do this? The Bible's answer is shame. We are ashamed of ourselves, and we don't want others to see what's really going on. Often there is something close to a soundtrack repeating in our head, saying, "They won't love you if they knew." The way of healing is to stop hiding. Only when we come out from behind the bushes do we deal shame a fatal blow. And where can we get the courage to confess? It comes from realizing that God already knows us inside and out and he still loves us. The courage comes from knowing the everlasting love of God expressed most clearly on the cross.

Father, give me the strength to step from behind the places where I'm hiding. I want to be honest. I want to be free. For this give me strength.

HEAL ME

A man with leprosy came to him and begged him on his knees, "If you are willing, you can make me clean." Jesus was indignant. He reached out his hand and touched the man. "I am willing," he said. "Be clean!"

MARK 1:40-41 NIV

In the ancient world, lepers were despised. No one was treated with more disdain. They couldn't go to the temple due to the risk of infecting others. They were shut off from family. They had to stay at a distance from others, yelling, "Unclean!" as they approached. It is said that rabbis wouldn't get closer than six feet from a leper.

The leper in Mark's gospel breaks code and walks up to the Rabbi Jesus. You can imagine the crowd gasping. And while Scripture says that Jesus was "indignant," it's clear that the indignation was not directed at the leper's audacity but at the condition he suffered. And then, with the crowd watching, Jesus touched the leper. It would have been easy to heal the man from a distance and then invite him closer. Even more, Jesus could have dismissed the leper for not following cultural protocol. Instead, Jesus said, "I am willing," and touched the man. Is there something keeping you at a distance from Jesus? Are you worried what might happen if you draw close? Are you paralyzed by what the crowd might think? Whatever is keeping you from him, know that he only wants to offer you his healing touch.

God, today I believe that you are willing to heal me. You desire to reach your hand toward me and say, "Be clean!"

NEEDING JESUS

Jesus said to them,
"It is not the healthy who need a doctor, but the sick.
I have not come to call the righteous, but sinners."
MARK 2:17 NIV

Can you imagine a hospital filled with people who don't need a doctor? A man in a stretcher alleging he can walk fine and doesn't need help. A young boy with a broken arm assuring a nurse that he doesn't need any help. These scenarios are pretty much unbelievable, but we don't feel the same way when imagining a church of people who think they're doing well and functionally don't need the Great Physician. That's much easier to believe. How tragic.

Early in his ministry, Jesus makes sure all who are listening understand that the whole reason he came was to heal and help—to rescue. That means two things. First, our relationship with God can't be based on our goodness but on confession of our need for Jesus. Any other way is laughable, like the sick man in the hospital pretending he's just fine. Second, followers of Jesus are called to build hospitals, not castles. Just like Jesus, we should seek out those who are in need, rather than protect ourselves from those who might have "issues." After all, every one of us needs the Great Physician; no one is beyond their need for Jesus.

Father, I confess my need for you again today. Jesus, I am just as in need of you now as I was ten years ago. Spirit of God, help me to love the sick around me like you love them.

STEP OUT IN FAITH

"But what about you?" he asked.
"Who do you say I am?"
Peter answered, "You are the Messiah."
MARK 8:29 NIV

When was the last time you risked something when you stepped out in faith? Maybe it was when you took a chance on a business venture or uttered the words, "I love you," for the first time. Maybe when you brought up a challenging conversation with an employer. Some find it easy to take these faith-filled steps while others are paralyzed by the pressure. Either way, often the only way forward in life is to take the step of faith.

Peter found himself in this situation when Jesus asked the disciples, "Who do you say I am?" Jesus hadn't forgotten who he was. He didn't need to be reminded of his name. Rather, he wanted them to step out in faith and boldly share who they believed he was. They had seen Jesus heal and teach, calm waters, and care for hurting people. Could he be the Messiah? was undoubtedly a question they had asked themselves, maybe even discussing it together, but Jesus wanted them to actually say it to him. It was Peter who had the courage and faith to speak what he had come to believe. So now he is remembered by his faith, while we don't know anything about what the others said at that point. As the proverb goes, "Fortune favors the bold." So, where is God calling you to step out in faith? In what is he inviting you to risk a bit?

God, you are in control. Help me believe that and to step out in faith.

AUGUST

In his kindness God called you to share in his eternal glory by means of Christ Jesus. So after you have suffered a little while, he will restore, support, and strengthen you, and he will place you on a firm foundation.

1 PETER 5:10 NLT

PARTICIPATING

When Jesus looked up and saw a great crowd coming toward him, he said to Philip, "Where shall we buy bread for these people to eat?" He asked this only to test him, for he already had in mind what he was going to do.

JOHN 6:5-6 NIV

Good leaders see needs before the needs present themselves. They anticipate and prepare for problems before they happen. Good leaders provide solutions, but great leaders invite others into the solution. Even if a leader can resolve the issue alone, there is value in having others participate in the action. Servant leaders don't have a "watch me" attitude. They increase effort and effectiveness by asking others, "What should we do?"

Before the feeding of the five thousand, Jesus invited his disciples into the miracle by asking Philip for his opinion. Jesus was fully capable of performing the miracle as a show for all to see, but he chose to use his disciples to be his hands and feet that day. As men and leaders, may we see the value in inviting others to be part of the miracles God desires to perform through us.

Lord God, thank you for inviting us into the story. Thank you for choosing me to participate in your work here on earth. May I invite others into the work you have called me to do as I serve you and your kingdom.

EMBRACING ABUNDANCE

"A thief has only one thing in mind—he wants to steal, slaughter, and destroy. But I have come to give you everything in abundance, more than you expect—life in its fullness until you overflow!"
JOHN 10:10 TPT

There are seasons of life when we struggle just to get by. There are also seasons when we are lulled into the trance of daily existence. Something deep within us knows that we were created for more than working jobs and paying bills. Something in our soul hungers for more than survival. But when the busyness of life hunts us down, we resort to managing life and controlling circumstances.

The roadway out of that routine is following Christ and accepting his offer of abundant life. If we receive the life that Jesus offers, we'll be able to bring life to those around us. To have something in abundance means to have more than enough. Experiencing abundant life is so much more than survival. Living abundantly doesn't only shape how we live; it shapes who we live for. When we have more life than we need, we'll create ways to give our lives away. We'll joyfully pour our lives into our families, our neighbors, or the strangers we meet, and we'll still have more to give.

God, help me to not settle for survival. Give me a heart that desires the abundant life you offer. Stir within me a spirit of generosity so I can joyfully bring life to those around me.

A NEW COMMANDMENT

"I give you a new commandment, that you love one another. Just as I have loved you, you also should love one another. By this everyone will know that you are my disciples, if you have love for one another."
JOHN 13:34-35 NRSV

If love becomes our default posture, we're heading in the right direction. If we choose love, we'll be following the new commandment Jesus gives us. But when we try to love one another with our own strength, we fall short of what Christ calls us to. Our greatest efforts of loving one another can only take us so far.

The love that Jesus loves us with comes from the Father. Christ explains the foundation of his love, saying, "As the Father has loved me, so I have loved you" (John 15:9). He then passes the love baton to us with the commandment to love one another. This love for others becomes a signpost of our commitment to Christ. The weight of loving one another is a lighter load to carry when we're filled with the Father's love for us. His love will fill in the gaps when our best efforts fail. When we tap into the unending supply of the Father's love, we will be able to love one another well.

Heavenly Father, your love for us stretches beyond the heavens. Your supply is more than enough. Fill my heart and soul with your love so I can love others more generously.

TO ALL PEOPLE

To the weak I became weak, that I might win the weak. I have become all things to all people, that by all means I might save some. I do it all for the sake of the gospel, that I may share with them in its blessings.

1 CORINTHIANS 9:22-23 ESV

Whether through a common interest or a shared hobby, a powerful connection can happen when we realize what unites us. Strong, lasting relationships are built when we celebrate the uniqueness of others and embrace the things we have in common. As our relationships develop, the needs of others become our needs, their struggles become our struggles, and their joys become our joys. Humility happens when we choose to leave our self-serving agendas to create the best opportunities for those around us.

When we grasp the blessings of the gospel, we will do what is necessary and become who we need to become so those around us can experience Christ in a life-changing way. The kingdom comes when we meet people where they are physically, emotionally, and spiritually. When people see our willingness to enter their world for the sake of the gospel and its blessings, doors are opened, walls come down, and people take a step closer to Christ and his kingdom.

God, increase my joy when I consider the blessings of the gospel. Give me courage to reach out to others for the sake of the gospel. May my character reflect yours as I seek to enter the lives of those around me.

GROWTH

We can all draw close to him with the veil removed from our faces. And with no veil we all become like mirrors who brightly reflect the glory of the Lord Jesus. We are being transfigured into his very image as we move from one brighter level of glory to another. And this glorious transfiguration comes from the Lord, who is the Spirit.

2 CORINTHIANS 3:18 TPT

Unlike our bodies, our spirits don't stop growing. And over time, as our bodies begin to deteriorate, our spirits are still being transformed into God's image. We don't arrive at a place in our faith journey where we are fully formed. With open hands and God's grace, we need to allow the Holy Spirit to guide our growth.

We are never too old, too weak, or too broken to reflect God's glory. If we get to a place where we're settling for suitable, we need to reclaim the childhood desire for growth. We need to pull ourselves out of the glory days and look forward to the next level of glory that the Lord wants to bring us to. We give others a glimpse of God's glory when we age but grow stronger, when our bodies break down but our spirits build up. As we reflect the glory of the Lord, may our hearts be open and our spirits ready.

Lord, continue to pour into my life so I can reflect your glory. Keep me humble. Make me willing. I am thankful that you are not done with me yet.

GIFT OF GRACE

God saved you by his grace when you believed.
And you can't take credit for this; it is a gift from God.
EPHESIANS 2:8 NLT

God's grace is a gift that has been paid for by Christ on the cross. The work we do in the name of Jesus, the service we render for the sake of the kingdom, should express our gratitude for that gift. We diminish the meaning of the cross when we attempt to earn God's grace through our works. If we have a spirit of entitlement, we cannot truly receive God's grace, because we believe it is owed to us. And if we believe we earned the gift, we expect others to do the same.

The biggest obstacle between the gift of grace and those who need to receive it from us, is the belief that we were the ones who paid for it. When we awaken to the reality that grace is a gift from God and that we did nothing to earn it, we can give it away with freedom and generosity. If we joyfully receive the gift, we will joyfully give it away to those around us. And when we extend grace to others amid their mistakes, they will walk away with a clearer understanding of the love that Christ has for them.

Lord, thank you for grace. Open my heart and my hands so I can freely receive and give the gift you have lavished upon me.

PURPOSE

We are God's masterpiece.
He has created us anew in Christ Jesus,
so we can do the good things
he planned for us long ago.
EPHESIANS 2:10 NLT

Our lives are not a made up of random events pieced together by the hands of time. We were created with intention and purpose by the hands of God. The Greek word poiema, which is translated "masterpiece," describes a work that only God can do. As an artist creating with intention, God has crafted us. He has made us as a beautiful depiction of the work he is doing in the world.

No two people are alike. Each of us is uniquely gifted to do the good works God has prepared for us to do. Crafting our history, weaving in our giftedness, and fastening our future, God continues to mold us for his purpose. He wants to use us to bring life to those around us and to encourage those under our care. When we embrace our uniqueness and live with purpose, we can confidently step into God's calling for our lives.

God, open my eyes to see what makes me unique. Help me discover my unique role in your kingdom. As I seek the good works you want me to step into, continue molding me to make me more like you.

TRUE POWER

Who, being in very nature God, did not consider equality with God something to be used to his own advantage; rather, he made himself nothing by taking the very nature of a servant, being made in human likeness. And being found in appearance as a man, he humbled himself by becoming obedient to death—even death on a cross!

PHILIPPIANS 2:6-8 NIV

If we want to be achievers in our culture, we need to commit to moving up the ladder of success. But no matter how high we climb, no matter what title we hold, we will never find ourselves being in very nature God. It is an honor to have a high position of power, but the challenge is found in how we use the position. If we have an attitude of entitlement, we will seek ways to have people meet our needs. If we have a spirit of humbleness, we will use our position of power to create ways to serve others.

Jesus relentlessly pursued the path of humility. This path led him beyond serving others and brought him to the cross. Committing to a life of humility will lead us to service and sacrifice. When we choose to pursue that path, we will find ourselves in good company.

God, give me the strength to pursue a path of humility. Help me see my life through a lens of humbleness, so I do not miss an opportunity to serve others.

FOCUS

Whatever is true, whatever is noble, whatever is right, whatever is pure, whatever is lovely, whatever is admirable—if anything is excellent or praiseworthy—think about such things.
PHILIPPIANS 4:8 NIV

It's often easier to focus on what's wrong with the world than it is to see the beauty around us. Our minds gravitate toward what needs fixing, what went wrong, or what could have been better. What we think about shapes what we see. The posture of our mind shapes how we experience life. If we're constantly thinking about what could go wrong, we'll see the shortfalls and identify the issues. If we have the posture of a critic, we'll pinpoint the problems.

But if we shift our focus, we can see and experience the beauty that has been hidden in plain sight. When we focus our minds on what is true, noble, right, pure, lovely, admirable, excellent, and praiseworthy, we will find something to celebrate. Thinking about those things helps improve our vision. We'll see the goodness in others more clearly and experience more joy in our lives.

God, shift my focus and sharpen my mind. Help me to think about all that is true, noble, right, pure, lovely, admirable, excellent, and praiseworthy so I can experience more joy in my life.

VISION

These all died in faith, not having received the things promised, but having seen them and greeted them from afar, and having acknowledged that they were strangers and exiles on the earth.
HEBREWS 11:13 ESV

When we live pursuing a vision, we sweep others into the movement. But we need to understand that the vision is of secondary importance to the pursuit. Hebrews explains that the people of faith did not receive the things promised. They did not see their vision fulfilled. Did that make them failures? Did that void their noble living? Did that make their lives a waste? Of course not.

If the vision itself is of primary importance, an unfulfilled vision voids all that precedes. In other words, if your dreams are dashed, your pursuit was a waste of time and effort. But if the dream is secondary to the pursuit, a strange thing happens. When you lose, you still win. If you don't get the championship ring, your dignity remains. If you don't get the job, your life is still intact. If your dream doesn't materialize, you can still inspire others to pursue theirs. Living in pursuit of a vision will shape how we live. If the pursuit of our vision is of primary importance, we can still inspire others to pursue their dreams even if we only greet ours from afar.

God, give me eyes to see that you surround me as I live in pursuit. May my pursuit inspire others to dream big and go after their vision.

SHEPHERDING

Care for the flock that God has entrusted to you. Watch over it willingly, not grudgingly—not for what you will get out of it, but because you are eager to serve God.

1 PETER 5:2 NLT

Life can provide many leadership opportunities for us, whether in the workplace, our churches, or amongst family and friends. As leaders, we have been put by God into a position that requires a high level of responsibility. He has made us shepherds of a flock. But there is freedom in understanding that our flock is ultimately his. He is the chief shepherd who entrusted a flock to us, and it is our role to nurture and care for that flock.

As we disciple our flock, our motives matter; we can't be selfish. Our attitude matters; we must be willing. Our focus matters and shapes how we care for our flock. When our priority is our flock, the weight of responsibility can overwhelm us. But if we shift our focus to God, the giver of the flock, we can trust that he will fill in where we fall short. When we trust the chief shepherd, who has called us into this role, we can eagerly serve him by caring for those entrusted to us.

God, thank you for the flock you have entrusted to me. As I disciple my flock, remove any selfish motives that are present. As I seek to serve you, instill a spirit of eagerness within me so I can serve with freedom and joy.

GOSPEL MESSENGERS

How beautiful on the mountains are the feet of the messenger who brings good news, the good news of peace and salvation, the news that the God of Israel reigns!

ISAIAH 52:7 NLT

We often think of missionaries as those who live in some far-off land. We look up to these people for their dedication and service, and we respect them for the sacrifices they make in order to bring the gospel to those in need.

When we walk across the street and share our faith with our neighbors, we are accomplishing the same goal as those missionaries working around the globe. Our calling to share the gospel with those around us is no less noble or important than the call of those serving in other areas. How can you be a messenger of the gospel in your neighborhood this week?

God, help me to be a messenger of the gospel. May I take every opportunity to share my faith with my neighbors and those within my community.

CEASE STRIVING

"Surrender your anxiety!
Be silent and stop your striving and you will see that I am God.
I am the God above all the nations,
and I will be exalted throughout the whole earth."
PSALM 46:10 TPT

We often see this verse translated "Be still, and know I am God." It hangs on banners in sanctuaries. It is quoted by well-meaning Sunday school teachers while trying to calm the squirrely boys and girls. This translation above, however, using "cease striving," speaks to the Father's heart.

We are constantly told how much more there is to do to be godly men. Work harder, love better: the pressure lies on our shoulders. But "cease striving and know that I am God" speaks to us. God is still God, and there is nothing that our striving can or will change about that. Have confidence that God is seated on his throne and know that sometimes we need to take a step back from our strivings to realize that.

God, help me to better understand your place on the throne, both of this world and of my heart. My strivings and work won't change that. Let me have confidence to stop striving after things that don't matter.

DISCIPLESHIP

It is the greatest joy of my life to hear that my children are consistently living their lives in the ways of truth!
3 JOHN 1:4 TPT

Few things bring us more joy and happiness than when we excel. That's why many of us participate in sports, learn an instrument, or pursue challenging careers. We seek out opportunities to achieve excellence. That's just what men do. As believers, we need to keep growing in our relationship with God. It seems obvious, but it's too important not to point out that our relationship with God is far more important than any other skill or achievement we could attain.

We can't will ourselves to follow Jesus any more than we can will ourselves to hit a ninety-mile-per-hour fastball, but we can do things to make sure we are exposed to the truth of God's Word. That might look like seeking out other men to hear about their faith stories or getting connected to a small group at a local church. However we choose to go about it, there's great joy to be found in pursuing truth alongside fellow believers.

God, thank you for the fellowship of believers. Help me to join others in pursuing a greater understanding of who you are. Help me to grow in my relationship with you.

FOCUS ON JESUS

We look away from the natural realm and we fasten our gaze onto Jesus who birthed faith within us and who leads us forward into faith's perfection. His example is this: Because his heart was focused on the joy of knowing that you would be his, he endured the agony of the cross and conquered its humiliation, and now sits exalted at the right hand of the throne of God!
HEBREWS 12:2 TPT

Keeping our eyes on Jesus sounds a lot easier than it really is. Our jobs, our family, our friends, our hobbies, our social contacts, and so much more are all fighting for our attention. There's no shortage of books and blogs that tell us what to believe and how we should be living our lives. Life often feels more like a car ride through a heavy rainstorm. The road becomes uncertain when we can't see more than a few feet ahead of us. We want to keep moving forward, but we can't see the familiar markers that tell us we're headed in the right direction. The only way it gets easier is if we're following the guiding taillights of someone ahead of us.

Jesus Christ has gone before us to make a way for us. If we can focus our eyes on him, he will lead us through the distracting storms of life and help bring clarity to our path. We fix our eyes on him when we spend time in his Word and prayer. Are your eyes fixed on him, or are you more focused on the worries you can't see?

God, you've made a way for me through your Son, Jesus Christ. Help me to not be distracted by other voices calling for my attention, but to fix my eyes on you, the author and perfecter of my faith.

REJOICING

The LORD your God is with you,
the Mighty Warrior who saves.
He will take great delight in you;
in his love he will no longer rebuke you,
but will rejoice over you with singing.
ZEPHANIAH 3:17 NIV

Do you remember being tucked into bed at night as a young boy? Most kids need to have their blankets just right and their stuffed animals all lined up perfectly. Parents will take a moment to say a prayer and often even sing a lullaby or two. It doesn't matter if the parents are good singers or not, kids absolutely love it! Their faces light up and they join in with the words. It's a special experience.

Even though many young parents may feel like they don't deserve this automatic devotion and delight of their young kids, it's truly a picture of how our Heavenly Father looks at us. He is like that parent tenderly singing over their little one whom they love. The child feels safe and trust is built as his parents affectionately care for him. We gain that same trust and security as God looks at us with joy and sings over us in love. Spend a moment thanking God for being your loving Father. Rest in child-like peace as you picture God singing over you.

God, thank you for the always being my Father. Thank you for the glimpse of your love for me, seen in an earthly dad with his little boy. Help me to know your love and to share it with those in my life.

MODELING

Brothers, join in imitating me, and keep your eyes on those who walk according to the example you have in us.
PHILIPPIANS 3:17 ESV

Do you have someone in your life who is worth following? Are there other men in your church who you look up to? How about men who love Jesus and live their lives for him? Paul says it simply: Follow their example.

Are you setting an example worth following for others? Would you be proud to have other men imitate your life? They are watching and learning. There are plenty of examples not worth following in our world. You have an opportunity, even an obligation, to set an example worthy of being followed.

God, thank you for the men you've placed in my life who have modeled a Christlike lifestyle for me. Help me to be that same example to others who are watching me.

APPROVAL

Am I now trying to win the approval of human beings, or of God? Or am I trying to please people? If I were still trying to please people, I would not be a servant of Christ.
GALATIANS 1:10 NIV

You can't please all people all the time, but we sure do like to try! Whether it be our friends, family, boss, or neighbor, we want the people in our lives to give us their seal of approval. And with that we worry. Are we saying the right things? Are we wearing the right clothes? If they knew what I really thought would they still accept me?

It's understandable that we want people to approve of us, but as servants of Christ we must take a different path. We will only experience true peace when it is God's approval that we pursue; and the things that God approves of often runs contrary to the ways of this world. So be prepared for conflict. But as we place God's opinion above the opinions of those around us, he will continue to draw us in, until we hear him utter the words, "Well done, good and faithful servant" (Matthew 25:21).

God, help me to seek your approval above man's.

THANKFULNESS

I will give thanks to the LORD with my whole heart;
I will tell of all your wonderful deeds.
I will be glad and exult in you;
I will sing praise to your name, O Most High.
PSALM 9:1-2 NRSV

What are you thankful for today? Is that an easy question to answer, or does it take time to think of something? Often, it's difficult for guys to articulate the things we're thankful for. It's not that we aren't thankful; we just don't always know how to verbalize it.

Take some time today to write down everything you're thankful for, no matter how small or big. Take time to talk with God and thank him for the things on your list. Then, tell someone else about your thankfulness for God's provisions. You'll be surprised at all you have to be thankful for and how verbalizing it helps you truly understand and feel your thankfulness.

God, help me to be a man with a thankful heart. Remind me of all I have to be thankful for, and help me be quick to share my thankfulness with others.

SELF-CONTROL

*I do not run aimlessly; I do not box as one beating the air.
But I discipline my body and keep it under control, lest after
preaching to others I myself should be disqualified.*
1 CORINTHIANS 9:26-27 ESV

Running aimlessly. When you read those words, what
picture forms in your mind? Do you see a marathon runner
aimlessly running a race? Imagine this man dragging his feet,
getting distracted by the crowd, and randomly stopping along
the way to check his phone. Now picture a focused runner in
the same race. His eyes are fixed straight ahead of him. He
can hear the crowd cheering him on, but he keeps a steady
footfall moving forward. He checks his watch, but only to make
sure he's at the pace he's trained for.

Are you living your life focused or aimless? Are you running
with a plan in place, or are you making things up as you go?
How can you discipline yourself to stay focused at the task at
hand?

**God, help me to run the race with focus and perseverance.
Remind me of what I am running for. May my actions be
worthy of the reward.**

JUSTICE

Speak up for those who cannot speak for themselves;
ensure justice for those being crushed.
PROVERBS 31:8 NLT

It's easy for us to show our support for those who are well-liked and respected. Showing our support for those who aren't as popular is much more difficult. Even so, it's our responsibility to speak up for those who cannot speak for themselves. The verse above describes ideas that the Old Testament king Lemuel learned from his mother. As king, Lemuel was put in a position of power and influence, so the words that his mother shared with him guided him as he guided others.

Do these words from king Lemuel guide our lives? Are we treating all people equally and speaking up for those who cannot speak for themselves? The way that we live our lives today will guide how others live their lives in the future.

God, help me to set an example of how to treat others. Help me to be a voice for those who cannot speak for themselves. Help me to set a legacy of justice.

LISTENING

Know this, my beloved brethren. Let every man be quick to hear, slow to speak, slow to anger, for the anger of man does not work the righteousness of God.
JAMES 1:19-20 ESV

Quick to hear, slow to speak, and slow to become angry. It's not natural, is it? Our instinct as men is to take control and fix things. We are quick to offer advice and criticism and quick to jump to conclusions. But this often leads to fighting, bitterness, and grudges.

James' words remind us of the importance of listening first and foremost. When we do this, we show that we care for the others involved in the conversation or situation. When we listen first, we remind ourselves that we're not the only ones who this affects. When we listen first, we aren't the experts. We aren't the ones trying to swoop in and fix everything with a quick answer.

God, help me to listen to those in my family, those at work, and those I'll interact with today. Help me to hear their story and respect them in my conversation.

PRAYER

Confess your sins to each other and pray for each other so that you may be healed. The prayer of a righteous person is powerful and effective.

JAMES 5:16 NIV

We could easily skip past the first part of this verse and jump straight to "the prayer of a righteous person is powerful and effective." That's the good stuff! We want to know that when we pray, it is going to be effective. We can't skip ahead though. The first part of this verse gives context to the second. James is reminding us of the importance of confessing our sins to one another. As men, we aren't good at that. We confess our sins to God in private prayers, but it's much more difficult for us to confess our sins to one another.

Confessing our mistakes and sin is not a form of weakness, but instead an example of righteousness. Are there people in your life to whom you need to confess? If so, make a plan today to do it.

God, thank you for the forgiveness that we have through your Son, Jesus Christ. Thank you that you promise that when we confess our sins to you, you are faithful to forgive. Help us to also confess our sins to those we have affected with our actions.

FREEDOM IN CHRIST

I do not understand my own actions. For I do not do what I want, but I do the very thing I hate. Wretched man that I am! Who will deliver me from this body of death? Thanks be to God through Jesus Christ our Lord.

ROMANS 7:15, 24-25 ESV

How many times have you found yourself saying these same words? You know what's best for you but just can't seem to follow through with it. Romans 7 records Paul's frustration with his inability to do the right thing. It's worth noting, though, the question that Paul asks: "Who will deliver me?" He doesn't ask what he needs to do or how he can try harder. Instead, he asks who can deliver him. Paul realized that there wasn't anything he could do on his own, but that he needed a Savior.

You're not good enough or strong enough to overcome your sin on your own. None of us are. But Jesus has already won the battle for you. Accept what he has done for you, and walk in victory through him.

God, you know my desire to do the right thing even though I continue to fall short of your standard. Help me to not try to be my own hero, but to fully accept what Jesus has done for me on the cross. Thank you that you have not only forgiven me but also freed me from the bondage of sin.

CONFIDENCE IN GOD

Great is our LORD, and mighty in power;
His understanding is infinite.
PSALM 147:5 NKJV

Have you ever wished you had someone to talk to who understood what you were going through? Sure, others are willing to listen, but they just don't understand. Have you ever wished that there was someone who could help bring clarity to your uncertainty?

This verse reminds us that God's understanding is infinite. The previous verse even says that he not only knows the number of stars in the sky but he calls them all by name. There is no feeling, situation, emotion, or problem that is beyond his comprehension. There's a whole list of qualities that we can ascribe to God, but have you thought of him as understanding? Approach him with confidence; you will not catch him off guard.

God, thank you that you are an understanding God. I take assurance in knowing that whatever I'm facing is not beyond your understanding. Help me to trust you with my uncertainty today.

PASSION

I am not ashamed of the Good News, because it is the power God uses to save everyone who believes—to save the Jews first, and then to save non-Jews.

ROMANS 1:16 NCV

We all have things we're passionate about: our favorite sports team, our preferred truck manufacturer, our love for bacon. These are things we love, and we are not ashamed of it.

But do we feel the same way about the gospel? Is it as easy for us to share with others the thankfulness we have for what God has accomplished in our lives through Jesus, as it is to talk about the stats from last night's game?

The gospel is God's power for salvation for all who believe! How can we proudly share our story of what the gospel has done for us with others today? How can we incorporate the importance of boldly living out and sharing the gospel into our daily lives?

God, please help me to see the need of the gospel in the lives of those I spend time with this week. Then help me to have the confidence I need to share the saving message of the gospel with them.

MENTORSHIP

*We loved you so much that we shared with you
not only God's Good News but our own lives, too.*
1 THESSALONIANS 2:8 NLT

Who are the people who've invested the most into you spiritually? It could be a father, a pastor, a Sunday school teacher, or a mentor. Chances are good that you've spent a fair amount of time with these people. They know you well, and you know them.

The verse above paints a beautiful picture of a mentor. Sharing God's good news is important, but so is sharing life. When you share your life with someone else, it builds trust. When you invite other people into your life, they get to observe you living out what you're sharing. Who are you sharing your life with? How are you sharing God's good news with them? By doing both, you're showing them that you truly love them.

God, help me to be a man who lives what I preach. Help me to not only tell others about you, but to invite them into my life so they can see me prioritizing your good news.

LEADERSHIP

*"As for me and my household,
we will serve the Lord."*
JOSHUA 24:15 NRSV

There are a lot of things that we don't have control over, and as men, that's scary. We want to be able to ensure we have a safe and secure environment to live in. But as we look around the world, it seems that much of it has turned its back on God.

We don't have control over the whole world, our country, or even our own community, but we do have control over what happens within our house. Today, will you commit to leading the way by serving the Lord? Will you teach others about who God is and how they can serve him?

God, I declare to you today that my desire is to be one that serves you. Help me to not lose focus on you, and to continue to put you first in everything that I do and say.

FATHERHOOD

"'Our Father, dwelling in the heavenly realms,
may the glory of your name
be the center on which our lives turn.'"
MATTHEW 6:9 TPT

When teaching his disciples to pray, Jesus started by addressing God as "Father." This authoritative definition that Jesus ascribes to God is the main image describing our relationship with God throughout the New Testament. It paints a beautiful picture of the nature of our relationship with God, as our father. Our earthly fathers are one of the most influential people in our lives, because they are meant to clearly model our relationship with God. They also have a direct impact on our understanding of God. Of course, men are fallible, and some fathers provide better examples than others.

What have we learned about our relationship with God through our experiences with our fathers? What can we learn from both the positive and negative examples they provided? These are questions that should both motivate us and draw us to our knees.

God, thank you for the privilege of knowing you as Father. Help me to understand this relationship more and more each day.

BUILDING A FOUNDATION

*Start children off on the way they should go,
and even when they are old they will not turn from it.*
PROVERBS 22:6 NIV

Your parents wanted the best for you, and so they did their best to teach and train you. They made sure you attended a good school, got you plugged into local church ministries, and set guidelines and expectations for you. And sometimes, they received pushback from you because of it.

It is important to remember, though, that they were not the ones who ultimately molded and changed your heart. That was the work of your heavenly Father. Their job was to start you off on the way you should go, that is, to point you toward Jesus in all circumstances. Your parent's window for influence in your life was limited, but God's work has barely just begun. Will you continue to build upon the foundation they have laid?

God, help me to stand firm on the foundation that has been set in my life. May I continue to build upon it with your truth and grace.

MOTIVATION

We always thank God for all of you and continually mention you in our prayers. We remember before our God and Father your work produced by faith, your labor prompted by love, and your endurance inspired by hope in our Lord Jesus Christ.

1 THESSALONIANS 1:2-3 NIV

Here we see Paul thanking God for the believers in Thessalonica. It's particularly interesting to see what Paul is thankful for: work produced by faith, labor prompted by love, and endurance inspired by hope in our Lord Jesus Christ. Their relationship with Christ influenced their daily life, and Paul noticed it.

When we allow our relationship with Christ to impact our whole life, our motivation changes. We live our life led by our faith in Christ. We begin to serve others out of a love that we have received from Christ. And we have the motivation to continue the work, even when it's difficult, because of the hope of eternity that we have in Christ. When we try to live our life apart from Christ, our work is just a job, an obligation that we need to fulfill. We tend to lose heart without hope. Is your life filled with faith, hope, and love, or is it marked by duty and obligation?

God, help me to be a man whose work is produced by my faith in you, and whose labor is prompted by my love for you and from you. May my endurance to continue be prompted by the hope for eternity that I have in Christ Jesus.

SEPTEMBER

My health may fail,
and my spirit may grow weak,
but God remains the
strength of my heart;
he is mine forever.

Psalm 73:26 NLT

ACCESS TO GOD

*In Christ we can come before God with freedom
and without fear. We can do this through faith in Christ.*
EPHESIANS 3:12 NCV

It's all about who you know, right? We all want to be that guy who has the connection to courtside seats at the big game, or the one who has the ear of the boss at work. The connections we make often come with benefits. How quickly we forget that we have direct access to God, the creator of the universe! We forget that we can speak with him, seek him for advice, and even ask him for help. And not only can we approach him, but he gladly welcomes us into his presence. We know that this is true only because of what Jesus Christ has accomplished for us on the cross.

Are you apprehensive about speaking to God? Do you feel like your issues or problems are too small to bother him with? Do you forget that we can speak to God and that he listens? Because of your relationship with Jesus, you can boldly approach him. Spend some time today just talking with God. He's looking forward to spending time with you!

God, thank you that I can come to you and speak to you. Thank you that I don't need an appointment or even a reason. Thank you that you listen to me and that you answer my prayers.

EFFECTIVE MINISTRY

Because you have these blessings, do your best to add these things to your lives: to your faith, add goodness; and to your goodness, add knowledge; and to your knowledge, add self-control; and to your self-control, add patience; and to your patience, add service for God; and to your service for God, add kindness for your brothers and sisters in Christ; and to this kindness, add love. If all these things are in you and are growing, they will help you to be useful and productive in your knowledge of our Lord Jesus Christ.

2 PETER 1:5-8 NCV

We all want to be effective. We want to be the best leaders, friends, teachers, and men that we can be. Very few people go through life just wanting to be average. In the verses above, Peter lists eight characteristics of an effective person. While it may be easy to see them as tasks to be completed, this isn't a list that will ever be completed in full. If we're to be effective, we need to "make every effort" (this will take work and time) to continue to grow in these areas.

Do you have more of these qualities in your life today than you did last week or last year? This is a list to be revisited. Whether this is your first year following Jesus or you've been following him for decades, it's important to continuously work on increasing your faith, goodness, knowledge, self-control, endurance, godliness, brotherly affection, and love.

God, help me to never feel like I have accomplished all that there is for me in you. May I continue to be intentional about growing in these qualities. Help me grow in my effectiveness as these qualities become more evident in my life.

FAITHFULNESS

You must honor the Lord and truly serve him with all your heart. Remember the wonderful things he did for you!
1 Samuel 12:24 NCV

What are some great things that God has done for you? Have you ever stopped to ponder his goodness in your life? Being thankful seems so simple, but we often forget the importance of remembering God's goodness and faithfulness in our lives. Find some time today to start a list of the great things that you've observed God doing in your life. Perhaps ask some friends or family members to brainstorm with you. To consider something is to carefully think about it. Don't just rush through your list to accomplish the task. Instead, carefully consider God's greatness in your life.

We are called to be men who "fear the Lord and worship him faithfully" with all our hearts. This becomes much easier to accomplish when we're regularly thinking about all the great things God is doing in our lives. As you lead in your various realms of influence, allow your thankfulness to God to lead you to be a man who fears and worships the Lord with all your heart.

God, your great works in my life are endless. Help me to never stop considering all the ways you're active and working in my life. May I live a life that is marked by my worship of you.

PERSONAL DEVOTION

Give yourselves completely to God. Stand against the devil, and the devil will run from you. Come near to God, and God will come near to you. You sinners, clean sin out of your lives. You who are trying to follow God and the world at the same time, make your thinking pure.

JAMES 4:7-8 NCV

There's only room for one leader in your life. We can't serve God and the evil one. It just doesn't work. James is pointing out our tendency to want to follow God but still give the devil authority in our lives. He says that we have to choose who we will follow.

Through Jesus, God has given us the ability to stand against the devil's temptations in our lives. We are no longer controlled by the power of sin. We have the ability to stand against sin and say no. James says that when we do this, the devil will run from us. When we decide to stand against the devil's schemes and instead draw near to God, not only will he draw near to us, but the devil and his temptations will also become less and less powerful in our lives.

God, help me to follow after you alone. Remind me of the victory that you have already accomplished over sin in my life through Jesus and give me the strength to stand against the devil in my life. Thank you for your promise to draw near to me as I draw near to you.

LOVING GOD

Loving God means keeping his commandments,
and his commandments are not burdensome.
1 JOHN 5:3 NLT

This sounds like a conversation our parents might have had with us when we were children: "If you love me, you will prove it by doing what I have asked you to do. I am not asking you to do anything that I know you can't do." We know that the best way for children to show their love for their parents is to do what they've asked of them.

It's no different for us. The best way we can show our love and appreciation for our heavenly Father is to follow the commandments he has given us. We display our love for him not just through the words we say to him but also by the way we live our lives. Actions truly do speak louder than words. How are you showing your love for your heavenly Father today?

God, I love you! Help me to live a life that displays my love for you through my obedience to you. Thank you that following your commands is possible for me because of the power of the Holy Spirit living within me.

SERVICE

As each has received a gift,
use it to serve one another,
as good stewards of God's varied grace.
1 PETER 4:10 ESV

God has uniquely gifted each of his children. He has created each of us with talents and abilities that are unique. As you look the people God has placed in your life, can you identify how each person has been gifted? How can you help them understand their giftings?

Once you have identified your giftings, it's time to discover how you can use your gifts to serve others, as individuals and in conjunction with other believers. God has not gifted each of us uniquely for our own benefit. Use your gifts to serve and help others. As you do, you'll discover that we are far stronger together than each person is alone.

God, thank you that I am created uniquely. Help me to use my gifts to serve others. Help me to be a good steward of what you have given me, and grant that, by my doing so, others might experience your love and grace.

EASTER

About three in the afternoon Jesus cried out in a loud voice, "Eli, Eli, lema sabachthani?" (which means "My God, my God, why have you forsaken me?").
MATTHEW 27:46 NIV

Men, this Easter reach down into your soul and let praise flow from your heart in singing praise to the King. Men have an issue with singing in church. Rumors of feminine influences and wishy-washy love songs about Jesus. The truth is we have been misinformed about what worship is. The New Testament teaches that worship is first a choice to engage. It's supposed to be an offering; in other words, it should cost. Then it's connected to the power of God on a mission. Mission and worship are inseparable.

Perhaps the most powerful place to see this demonstrated was on Calvary's cross. Jesus—hanging on that old wooden tree, having chosen to engage—brought a costly offering, his very life. He meaningfully took part in the very mission of God. This bloodied and beaten Savior, crucified and dying, lifted his voice and sang in worship. He worshiped his father with Psalm 22. Men, if you ever doubt the masculinity of worship, the man Jesus, hanging by nails to a cross, finds within his heart a desire to sing praise to God. This Easter, let's not make excuses. Let's make a joyful noise.

Lord, I repent of my worship attitude. Forgive me for making it about me. Help me engage and worship you.

LIVING UP TO OUR WORTH

As a prisoner for the Lord, then, I urge you to live a life worthy of the calling you have received. Be completely humble and gentle; be patient, bearing with one another in love. Make every effort to keep the unity of the Spirit through the bond of peace.
EPHESIANS 4:1-3 NIV

Do parents set rules and guidelines for their children to follow so they'll love them more? Do they place expectations on them so they can earn their love? No. they love them and want to see them succeed. They have set standards for them because they know what they're capable of and they want to see them achieve their full potential.

When Paul says to "live a life worthy of the calling that you have received," he's not saying that these are things we need to do to earn God's love or to prove ourselves to him. Instead, he is making it clear that we have received the high calling of being a child of God and that we should be living our lives in a way worthy of such a calling. When you think about your life, do the words humble, gentle, patient, bearing with one another in love, and unity describe you? These are the qualities present in a life that is living up to the high calling it has received. Allow these words to motivate you to a higher standard of living not so you can earn God's favor, but so you can live up to what God already sees in you.

God, thank you for the value you see in me. Thank you that you've called me to be your son. Help me to live in a way that reflects the life you have called me to.

ATTITUDE

Rejoice in the Lord always; again I will say, rejoice.
Let your reasonableness be known to everyone.
The Lord is at hand.
PHILIPPIANS 4:4-5 ESV

It's easy to rejoice when things are going well. When you receive that job promotion that you've been waiting for, or when your bank account reaches a new high. But how can we rejoice when it doesn't seem natural? How do we rejoice when we lose our job, the furnace goes out and we don't have money to replace it, we're constantly fighting with a friend, or we receive news from the doctor that cancer is affecting us or someone we love?

Paul understood that rejoicing in the Lord wasn't always easy or natural. After all, he wrote these words while sitting in a prison cell. Thankfully, he does cast some light on how it is possible: "The Lord is at hand." Paul reminds us of the Lord's promise that he is with us always. We can rejoice in knowing that God is aware of our circumstances and that he is with us, just as he was with Paul in that prison cell. As you face each new day, do so with an attitude that rejoices in the Lord in all circumstances. As you do, you are modeling your trust in the Lord's provisions for everyone to see.

God, thank you for the promise of your presence in my life. Remind me of your presence when things are difficult. Help me rejoice in you always.

GODLINESS

Man of God, flee from all this, and pursue righteousness, godliness, faith, love, endurance and gentleness. Fight the good fight of the faith. Take hold of the eternal life to which you were called when you made your good confession in the presence of many witnesses.

1 TIMOTHY 6:11-12 NIV

As a child, do you ever remember your parents saying to you, "That's not how we do it in this family"? They wanted you to know that the standard your family holds to is different from the standard you saw around you. They wanted you to know that because you are a part of their family, you are held to a higher standard. That's the kind of conversation Paul is having with Timothy. He is reminding him about his identity as a child of God. Timothy is called to a greater standard of living. Paul calls him to action with words like flee, pursue, fight, and take hold. He is reminding him that being a child of God requires action, that he can't just expect these things to happen to him.

The same is true for you. You are a child of God, and you've been called to a high standard of living that's only realized with a commitment to action. Flee from the evil that is around you and pursue what is good. Be willing to fight for your faith. As you do this, keep in mind the end destination: eternal life with Christ.

God, thank you for the reminder that I am your child. Thank you that you have not only called us to a higher standard, but that you are also empowering us to victory as we pursue and fight for our faith.

STRENGTH IN WEAKNESS

He said to me, "My grace is sufficient for you,
for my power is made perfect in weakness."
Therefore I will boast all the more gladly of my weaknesses,
so that the power of Christ may rest upon me.
2 CORINTHIANS 12:9 ESV

We aren't all that willing to admit our weaknesses, are we? We don't like to confess that we get lost while driving, much less that we are struggling. We are men and people are counting on us. We can do this on our own. We have to. Right? Wrong.

It's time we rid ourselves of that mentality and embrace the fact that we aren't the superhero we sometimes believe we need to be. It's time we realize that we lead best when we allow God's grace and power to be evident in our lives. We are strongest when we lead and live with a dependence on God's work in our lives. As he has said, "My grace is sufficient for you, for my power is made perfect in weakness." Let's make room for God's power by admitting that we can't do it all on our own.

God, forgive me for wanting to do things my way and on my own. Forgive me for not seeking help when I need it, from others or from you. Help me to admit my weaknesses to you today. I invite you to come and work in my life.

THANKFULNESS

Oh give thanks to the LORD;
call upon his name;
make known his deeds among the peoples!
PSALM 105:1 ESV

One of the first things we are taught to say is, "Thank you." Our parents wanted us to know the importance of having a thankful heart. So we were taught to send thank-you notes for gifts, say thank you to our hosts, and to say a prayer of thanks before a meal. In God, we have so much to be thankful for. This verse instructs us to not just say thank you to God for all that he has done for us, but also to tell others of our thankfulness. We are to "make known his deeds among the peoples."

Today, what can you share with others about what God has done for you? How can you share your thankfulness to God with your family and friends?

God, thank you for your many blessings in my life and in the lives of my family. Help me to be quick to share and tell others of all that you've done.

GOD IS GREATER

The foolishness of God is wiser than human wisdom,
and the weakness of God is stronger than human strength.
1 CORINTHIANS 1:25 NIV

It seems strange to read about God's foolishness and weakness. But what Paul is trying to help us understand is that in all things and in every way, God is greater. We live in a do-it-yourself world where many of us want to figure things out on our own. We think that if we ask for help, we're admitting that we are weak. This verse reminds us that even at our greatest and strongest, we still don't compare to God.

Isn't it encouraging to know that God is not only wise and strong, but that he is also on our side? We can confidently come to him, knowing that he is more than sufficient to help us in every situation we will ever find ourselves in. And likewise, when others come to us for help, we can do our best to guide them by pointing them to God.

God, help me to rest in your strength and your wisdom. Help me to trust you to help me and not try to accomplish everything in my own strength. Thank you for the wisdom and strength that you gladly share with your children.

LEADERSHIP

"Do to others what you would want them to do to you."
LUKE 6:31 NCV

Sometimes it's the simple things in life that make the most sense. The idea behind the verse above is taught in preschools all over the world. But it is no less true in our homes, businesses, and lives. Do to others what you want done to you. Are you modeling the behavior you want to see in those you have authority over? It's easy to want to lead out of power and authority, but the best way for us to lead is through treating others the way we wish to be treated.

People will often listen to our words, but they're more likely to follow our example. People are watching you. They will follow the behaviors, attitudes, and actions that they see modeled for them. Are your words of instruction also being lived out in your own life?

God, thank you for this simple reminder today. Help me to live my life in a way that is worthy of being replicated by those around me. Help me to lead by example in the way that I treat and interact with others.

CONTENTMENT

Keep your life free from love of money,
and be content with what you have,
for he has said, "I will never leave you nor forsake you."
HEBREWS 13:5 ESV

As men, we want to be the ones who provide for ourselves. We want to not only get what we need but also what we want. Who doesn't want things that are fun? So how we can find contentment even without the things that money can buy? How can we help others to understand contentment in what they have? The answer begins with understanding who God is.

God is our creator, our provider, our sustainer, and our defender, and he is deeply in love with us. When we have a right understanding of who God is and what he does for us, our priorities and values begin to change. Knowing that God has promised to never leave or forsake us should bring comfort. We can do our best to provide for ourselves, but we should also know that God has promised to care for us. He will provide.

God, help me to rest in the promise of your never-ending presence in my life. May I value your presence more than the love of money or possessions in my life.

GRACE AND FORGIVENESS

Make allowance for each other's faults,
and forgive anyone who offends you.
Remember, the Lord forgave you,
so you must forgive others.
COLOSSIANS 3:13 NLT

Forgiveness and grace are powerful things. Along with love, they could probably fix almost any problem in any part of the world. That sounds like a bold statement, doesn't it? Consider a situation in your life. If you went to someone and asked for forgiveness or granted forgiveness, what would happen? How would it change the dynamics of that relationship?

When the apostle Paul uses the word allowance, it sounds like a directive to expect faults and mistakes. He realizes the nature of the church and relationships and how messy they can be. We never intend for them to get messy, but we get tired, we become frustrated when the bank account isn't where we want it to be, we lose our jobs, and we are affected by everyday life. We expect people to make allowances for us, so we should do the same through the power of the grace of God.

God, help me to remember that you grant me grace. You forgive my faults. Now give me the ability to do the same for the people in my life.

DELIGHT IN GOD

*Take delight in the L*ORD*,*
and he will give you your heart's desires.
*Commit everything you do to the L*ORD*.*
Trust him, and he will help you.
PSALM 37:4-5 NLT

Something unique happens when we delight in God. It's one thing to delight in a certain kind of food or a hobby or even a job. But it's altogether different when we delight in God, because he starts to plant within us new desires; desires for more of him, for more love, peace, grace, and the list goes on. As a man, if you delight in God, then he will start to shape your desires to be in alignment with his. You'll begin to be committed to him with every aspect of your life. True commitment to God will inform how you see yourself and others. It doesn't necessarily make life easier, but it certainly gives you wisdom, grace, and perspective for whatever comes your way.

If our vehicle seems out of sorts, we take it to a mechanic. If our own life and faith seems out of sorts, we need to recalibrate ourselves in relation to God and recommit ourselves to him.

God, in this moment I commit myself, as well as my desires, to you. Help me to be in alignment with your will for my life.

GOD'S WILL

This is what the LORD says: "You will be in Babylon for seventy years. But then I will come and do for you all the good things I have promised, and I will bring you home again. For I know the plans I have for you," says the LORD. "They are plans for good and not for disaster, to give you a future and a hope."

JEREMIAH 29:10-11 NLT

Often, verse 11 of Jeremiah 29 gives people a sense of excitement about their future because they can see that God has plans for good. But how often do we forget what verse 10 says? They will be in captivity for "seventy years." God lets his people know that the future is bright, yes; but his will doesn't necessarily change circumstances overnight.

As men, sometimes we just want to know what the plan is and then we are settled. But we must also realize that the plan may include a process. We want to understand things right away, but we must recognize that God is patient with us because we too are in process. Sometimes God even allows the process to take longer than we might like. Trust this day that God has great plans and a will for you, and also know that it's a process. Even though it doesn't seem like much is happening, that doesn't mean God isn't working.

God, help me to trust your will for my life. Give me the ability to be okay with the process.

REMOVE THE CLUTTER

"Blessed are the poor in spirit,
for theirs is the kingdom of heaven."
MATTHEW 5:3 NIV

When Jesus is speaking to an audience that is already poor, it seems odd to be encouraging even more poverty. The words "poor in spirit," however, speak to more than just an economic status, although that is a part of it. Ultimately, what matters is that when one's life is void of clutter, there is a greater awareness of God. When everything is stripped away, a new level of trust in God is experienced physically, spiritually, mentally, financially, and emotionally.

Jesus encourages his followers to be drawn into a deeper level of trust. As men, sometimes we can fill our lives with so much clutter or activities that we're unable to sift through what really matters at a much deeper level. Consider what you might need to strip away from your life. How can you model a life of simplicity for others so they understand what it means to be poor in spirit?

God, draw me into a deeper relationship with you, and help me to remove the clutter so I can trust even more in you.

GENEROSITY

"When you give to the needy, do not let your left hand know what your right hand is doing, so that your giving may be in secret. And your Father who sees in secret will reward you."
MATTHEW 6:3-4 NIV

Doesn't it often seem like there is that guy at the party who can't stop talking about himself? All the places he's been, all the extreme stunts he's accomplished and all the people in need that he rescued. But in the end, his boasting often leaves us feeling a bit sorry for his hidden insecurity, rather than placing him on the pedestal he's trying to reach. IN the same way, when someone starts talking about the overly generous donation that they gave, we are left questioning the true intentions behind their gift.

Jesus talked about the rich, the poor, and money a lot. Giving always seemed to be a top priority for him; he even gave his life. Generosity can feel easier said than done. Sometimes in our life of surrender to the Lord, our wallet is the final thing handed over to Jesus. When we do give in secret, or simply without the fanfare, we are confident in the reward and pleasure of the Father over us. Whether it's writing a check to our church or giving of our time at the local food bank, there is no need to let everyone know. It's our choice, do we want God to be glorified or man's empty praise?

God, help my heart to be in alignment with the heart of Jesus. Cultivate a heart for the poor within me that would lead to generosity.

MONEY

"Don't store up treasures here on earth, where moths eat them and rust destroys them, and where thieves break in and steal. Store your treasures in heaven, where moths and rust cannot destroy, and thieves do not break in and steal. Wherever your treasure is, there the desires of your heart will also be."
MATTHEW 6:19-21 NLT

Do you remember ever hearing children comparing their dads to other dads? They might say, "Well, my dad has this kind of car," or "Oh yeah, well, my dad has this kind of car." One-upping is an art form that continues to this day.

It's so easy to fall into the trap of wanting all the "right" stuff, the "right" toys, and the "right" amount of money. Jesus warns against this kind of idolatry, because he recognizes the toll it takes on our heart and soul. It shows who we really are and what we really desire. Take some time today to think about how you view money and possessions, and what really matters to you.

God, help me to not make money and possessions idols in my life. I confess that I often put too much stock in "things." Help me to put my trust in you even more today.

PROVIDENCE

"Do not worry, saying, 'What shall we eat?' or 'What shall we drink?' or 'What shall we wear?' For the pagans run after all these things, and your heavenly Father knows that you need them. But seek first his kingdom and his righteousness, and all these things will be given to you as well."
MATTHEW 6:31-33 NIV

Providing for yourself can be one of the most rewarding, and yet most worrisome, responsibilities a man can have. The moment we get our first job, we start to think about our needs on a whole new level. It can also give us even more perspective on the verses above. If we think this much about providing for ourselves, how much more does God think about providing for us!

But the reality is that providing for ourselves can be a daunting task. What if we lose our job? What if an unforeseen bill comes in the mail? Whatever the case, it seems the way of Jesus is to not worry. That is truly easier said than done, but it's not impossible. Be present in each moment, and plan to the best of your ability, but know ultimately that God will provide. It may not be as you imagined it, but as you cultivate a life of faith, you grow into the habits of a life free from worry.

God, give us this day our daily bread. Help me to trust that you will provide for me.

PERSISTENT PRAYER

"Keep on asking, and you will receive what you ask for. Keep on seeking, and you will find. Keep on knocking, and the door will be opened to you. For everyone who asks, receives. Everyone who seeks, finds. And to everyone who knocks, the door will be opened."

MATTHEW 7:7-8 NLT

Jesus tells us that our heart's motivation in prayer, as we seek the Holy Spirit, is persistence. Keep on! We are promised that as we seek God, we will find him every time. Prayer might seem like a challenging thing at times, but as you keep on praying, you will grow—guaranteed.

For today's devotion, consider how you can pray for the people in your life. What do they need? How do you see them growing? What do you like about them? What gifts are they developing? Ask God to help them grow in that gift. Or maybe a time of prayer looks like five minutes of silence. Seeking God can be done in silence and solitude as well.

God, help me to grow in prayer. Teach me how to pray for my kids. Remind me what I love about them.

KINGDOM OF GOD

Here is another illustration Jesus used: "The Kingdom of Heaven is like a mustard seed planted in a field. It is the smallest of all seeds, but it becomes the largest of garden plants; it grows into a tree, and birds come and make nests in its branches."

MATTHEW 13:31-32 NLT

Jesus often talked about the kingdom of God or the kingdom of heaven. It's much greater and richer than an afterlife destination; it's a way of life. It's the reason Jesus asks us to pray that his kingdom would come on earth as it is in heaven. When you think of living in the way of Jesus, the kingdom of heaven, what comes to mind? Jesus is often comparing it to something small and seemingly insignificant, but over time (perhaps a long period of time) it grows and has purpose.

In the illustration above, Jesus talks about the kingdom of heaven being a home or a refuge. In a lot of aspects, our transition from childhood to manhood can be modeled after this illustration. It starts out in simple ways, but over time our relationships with others grows and changes. The question is, does it grow into something with purpose? As a man, are you a safe refuge for those in your life?

God, develop me into the man you want me to be. Help me to pattern my life after the way of Jesus, and may your kingdom come.

POSSESSIONS

Jesus told him, "If you want to be perfect, go and sell all your possessions and give the money to the poor, and you will have treasure in heaven. Then come, follow me."
MATTHEW 19:21 NLT

In Western culture, consumerism is the air we breathe. We have holidays that celebrate getting more—more stuff. We love stuff, and it's hard to think of life outside those terms. Whenever we find ourselves in a store, we are bombarded with the same idea—to get more.

Yet Jesus appeals to a different kind of living. He attributes a desire for perfection to getting rid of stuff. He calls his followers to a life of simplicity and getting rid of things that can dominate our life. He recognizes that we sometimes even organize our lives and our calendars around our stuff. We purchase extra storage units to become a house for our stuff, and all the while our heart is more and more cluttered and has no room to be mindful of God, much less those who have virtually nothing. As a man, following Jesus looks like a life of simplicity and generosity. Think about how you can model this kind of living for those around you.

God, help me to declutter my life so I am wholly devoted to you.

LEAD THROUGH SERVING

It should not be that way among you. Whoever wants to become great among you must serve the rest of you like a servant.
MATTHEW 20:26 NCV

When Jesus appealed to his disciples about leadership, status, and positions of power, he gave them an upside-down way of thinking. He said the best leaders are the ones that not only know how to serve but actually participate in serving. When we are young, sometimes it seems like we're constantly being served because we can't do things ourselves. But over time, if our parents aren't intentional about giving us responsibility, we will expect others to keep serving us. It's a challenging balance to not only be a servant but also encourage others to adopt an attitude of service as well.

One of the best ways to model this kind of leadership is to get out and find a way to serve within your community, whether it is volunteering at a soup kitchen, a homeless shelter, or perhaps your local church. The best leaders are the ones who are willing to get their hands dirty and serve.

God, help me to model a life of joyful servitude as I continue to grow as a humble servant leader.

INVESTMENT

"His master replied, 'Well done, good and faithful servant! You have been faithful with a few things; I will put you in charge of many things. Come and share your master's happiness!'"
MATTHEW 25:21 NIV

In Matthew 25, Jesus tells an interesting parable about a master who gives three different servants various amounts of money. Two of them invest their amount and it grows, while the third servant buries it. This parable can have multiple meanings, but one of the most popular applications is the idea of investment. It's not just concerning our finances, although that is an important aspect; it's also important to consider our gifts and talents as well.

Are you using the gifts God has given you to invest in and make a difference in the world? How do you invest in the lives of others? Today, think of one way that you can make an investment in someone else's life. The reward of your investment is invaluable.

God, thank you for investing in me by sending Jesus so I can be in relationship with you. Help me to understand more of what my gifts are, so that I can invest them into others.

A LIFE OF SACRIFICE

"Greater love has no one than this:
to lay down one's life for one's friends."
JOHN 15:13 NIV

As men, we've heard so many times that being "tough" or "strong" looks like standing our ground, not letting our emotions get the best of us, and having a stiff upper lip. These ideas were constructed by different cultures over time, but they are not the way of Jesus. Being a man—even more, a man of God—involves love, sacrifice, and friendship. We could say the truest man was revealed in the person and character of Jesus. He was a man who deeply loved people. The disciples weren't just his followers or students; they were together for nearly three years. We must assume they became close friends, and then one day he made the ultimate sacrifice. He lost his friends, and they lost him. But the sacrifice was far greater than anyone would realize.

What does sacrifice look like for you as a man? How can you show true love today? Maybe it looks like setting aside your desires and putting someone else's needs first. Maybe it's something much bigger and more complex. How can you show love in these situations?

God, thank you for making the ultimate sacrifice for me. Help me to live a life of sacrifice.

THE HOLY SPIRIT

"When the Spirit of truth comes, he will guide you into all truth. He will not speak on his own but will tell you what he has heard. He will tell you about the future."
JOHN 16:13 NLT

We all experience various levels of partnerships in our life, whether with friends, coworkers, or family members. But there's another partner that we can also rely on—the Holy Spirit. It's important and sometimes challenging to cultivate a relationship with earthly partners; we could say the same for our relationship with the Holy Spirit. As you deepen your relationship with God, ask that you'll also be continuously filled with the Holy Spirit. It'll serve as sort of a road map for your faith life as well as your parenting life. (Even though men stereotypically don't like to use maps, right?)

Another name for the Holy Spirit is "Counselor." Take some time right now to consider God as a counselor: one who listens and one who comforts. What do you need to get off your chest? What are you struggling with? In what areas do you need direction, guidance, or comfort?

God, continue to fill me with your Holy Spirit. Lead me into truth: the truth of who you are, as well as the truth of who I am.

FEAR OR TRUST

"The Lord is on my side; I will not fear.
What can man do to me?"
PSALM 118:6 ESV

Fear can be packaged in many ways. Sometimes it may look like you or a loved one getting sick; other times it might be financial instability, or it could even take the guise of a natural disaster. As men, we might struggle with how to deal with fear in our life. Perhaps we view fear as weakness, and we definitely don't want to be viewed as weak. Why would the Bible instruct us to not fear when the reality is everyone encounters fearful situations in life? Fear is part of the human experience, but praise God that he has provided the antidote: Trust. When dark clouds loom overhead and the future looks bleak, do we trust that the Lord is on our side? When the diagnosis is grim and healing is nowhere to be found, do we trust that the Lord is on our side? When the ground beneath us shakes and the mountains crumble into the sea, do we trust that the Lord is on our side?

As Christians, our answer is a resounding yes! If we can live with the perspective that the Lord, the all-powerful creator and sustainer of all things, is on our side, what could this world ever do to us? This doesn't mean that we will never experience fear in our lives, but the fear that we do encounter will fade away as it is eclipsed by our trustworthy Father.

God, you are a trustworthy father. Help me to recognize that fear cannot be sustained in the blinding light of your presence.

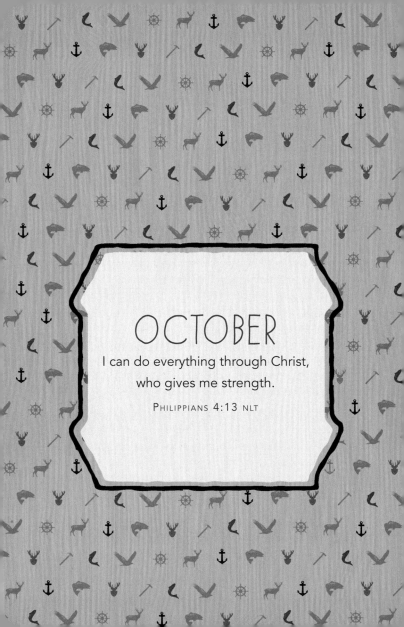

OCTOBER

I can do everything through Christ,
who gives me strength.

PHILIPPIANS 4:13 NLT

COMPARISON

When Peter saw him, he said to Jesus,
"Lord, what about this man?" Jesus said to him,
"If it is my will that he remain until I come,
what is that to you? You follow me!"
JOHN 21:21-22 ESV

Sometimes it's easy to look at others and compare our situation to theirs. With other men we might compare salaries, home sizes, car styles, and the list goes on. We frequently wonder how we stack up. We might say, "At least I'm better than that person," or "If only I were as good as that person." It's a constant game of comparison, and we start young.

When Jesus was talking to Peter about Peter's life, Peter wanted to compare his future with that of another disciple. Jesus basically says, "It's not your concern, Peter. Be concerned about Peter—about yourself! You follow me." It seems the best cure for comparison is simply turning to Jesus and following him. Think about what comparisons you might be making in your own life, particularly as a man. How can you turn your attention back to Jesus?

God, help me to follow you and focus on you. May I turn away from the temptation to compare myself with others.

COMMUNITY

They devoted themselves to the apostles' teaching and the
fellowship, to the breaking of bread and the prayers.
ACTS 2:42 ESV

It seems that the early followers of Jesus found it imperative to form a community after his death, resurrection, and ascension. They focused on just a few things that they devoted themselves to regularly. We eventually started calling this community "church," except that church has taken on many different forms over the last two thousand years or so.

Ultimately, community is essential for followers of Jesus. Are you plugged into a community? It doesn't matter the size or the building; what matters is togetherness and breaking bread and devoting yourselves to learning about God in the Scriptures. If you are currently attending a church, is it causing you to grow in your faith?

God, help me to continue to be part of a community that is enriching for me. Even when it gets hard, help me to strive toward unity.

SHAME

There is now no condemnation for those who are in Christ Jesus, because through Christ Jesus the law of the Spirit who gives life has set you free from the law of sin and death.
ROMANS 8:1-2 NIV

As men, sometimes when we think about our actions, it can bring great pride, great shame, or perhaps something in between. And sometimes when we fail at something or make a mistake, we might think that we are failures. First and foremost, the apostle Paul tries to make it clear to us that as we find our worth and identity in Christ, we are encouraged to not put any additional and unnecessary shame on ourselves for the brokenness we experience in the world. Once we find our identity in Christ, we recognize that we need grace upon grace.

We need to embrace this way of thinking. We should expect to make mistakes. We are going to experience brokenness. That doesn't mean that we are failures as men or followers of Christ. Do your best to provide a grace-filled environment for yourselves. When we make mistakes, do not embrace shame but instead receive the grace that Jesus provides. And then talk about the mistake. What can we learn from it?

God, grant me grace for every situation I encounter today.

TRUST

We know that God causes everything to work together for the good of those who love God and are called according to his purpose for them.
ROMANS 8:28 NLT

We usually reference the above verses when something bad happens, so we can have hope amid our potentially negative circumstances. Just a few verses before this, the apostle Paul appeals to our weaknesses. This all certainly applies to difficult things that we may have already experienced, but a handful of the verses in this chapter deal with the future tense as well. It's almost as if he is telling us to prepare our hearts for whatever comes our way and to ultimately know that when (not if) life gets hard, God is still working.

Even when your health is poor, God is still working. Even when your job is in jeopardy, God is still working. Even when you can't seem to get along with those around you, God is still working. If you love God, you can trust him knowing that he is still working.

God, help me to trust you even when things get hard, and please keep working on me, in me, and around me.

TRANSFORMATION

*Do not conform to the pattern of this world, but be
transformed by the renewing of your mind. Then you will
be able to test and approve what God's will is—his good,
pleasing and perfect will.*
ROMANS 12:2 NIV

It's easy to get distracted by what we see and hear in
culture about how we should live our lives, how to make
money, how to lose weight, how to gain weight, what to buy,
what not to buy, and the list goes on. None of these things are
inherently bad to consider, but in the verse above, the apostle
Paul is concerned about the ways of culture dominating every
thought we have and controlling us.

Transformation requires a move of God not only in your
heart but also in your mind. Renewal is needed within your
thought life so you can suppress the cultural distractions and
instead focus on God. What kind of mind shift needs to happen
for you to see God more clearly today? How can you begin (or
continue) to think about your life in a God-honoring way?

**God, help me to give not just my heart and soul to you, but
my mind as well. Continue to renew my thoughts.**

A STRONG FOUNDATION

"Everyone who hears these words of mine and puts them into practice is like a wise man who built his house on the rock. The rain came down, the streams rose, and the winds blew and beat against that house; yet it did not fall, because it had its foundation on the rock."

MATTHEW 7:24-25 NIV

The storms of life can come from any and every direction. It is during these storms that our foundation is tested. The stronger the storm, the greater the test. Jesus painted a picture of a storm that hit from all angles. The rain came down, the streams rose, and the winds blew and beat against the house. But the foundation was solid and the house withstood the storm. The foundation was not built during the storm; it was built before the winds picked up. It was not made by the storm; it was made for the storm.

Jesus explains that the foundation of our faith is built through action. It is not built on hearing God's Word but being obedient to it. It is built by taking the words of Christ and putting them into practice. Before you go through difficult days, you need to do the hard work of obedience and build a strong foundation that can weather the storm.

Lord, help me rely on you before the difficult days. Guide me as I build a strong foundation of faith in you. When the rains come, help me stand with courage and confidence.

FRUIT OF THE SPIRIT

*The Holy Spirit produces this kind of fruit in our lives: love, joy,
peace, patience, kindness, goodness, faithfulness, gentleness,
and self-control. There is no law against these things!*
GALATIANS 5:22-23 NLT

Often, when trying to rely on our own strength and will
power to be men of God, we fall short. Jesus embodied the
kind of person we all hope to become. God recognizes this
need we have, and so he sent his Spirit to not only guide us
and lead us into truth, but to also develop character within us.
A good fruit tree is planted in good soil, watered, trimmed if
necessary, and given the right amount of sunlight.

Much like a fruit tree, we require a good foundation and
proper care. We require the Holy Spirit as followers of Jesus. If
we find ourselves to be people (and men) who follow Jesus but
aren't exhibiting any of the qualities above, perhaps we need
to ask God to continue to fill us with the Holy Spirit. If you've
never done that before, take a moment and pray for it now.

**God, fill me with your Holy Spirit today so I can become
more and more like Jesus Christ.**

PROCESS

I am sure of this, that he who began a good work in you will bring it to completion at the day of Jesus Christ.
PHILIPPIANS 1:6 ESV

Sometimes we want instant gratification. Things need to happen right now. In our age of greater technology, everything is available at the click of a button, and when this becomes the norm, we project this mentality onto every aspect of our lives without even thinking about it.

That includes our relationship with God and our relationship with others. It's hard to find stories in the Bible where a person has an encounter with God and immediately becomes a complete person. Even the apostle Paul. When he said yes to God, he was still blinded temporarily. He went through a process to become the man God intended him to be. Even after lots of ministry, Paul still confessed his issues and areas of growth. We should expect that our lives are a process. They are not microwaved. So don't feel rushed or like you're behind. Are you where you ultimately want to be with God or in your relationships? Maybe not, but are you in a different place today than you were yesterday or a year ago? Most likely.

God, help me to be patient with the process and know that you're transforming me to be more like Jesus.

ATTITUDE

You must have the same attitude that Christ Jesus had.
PHILIPPIANS 2:5 NLT

Science and experience have shown us that at a very early age, people start imitating those around them: their mannerisms, their speech patterns, even their facial expressions. It can be fun to watch and sometimes a little scary too. And as we grow and spend even more time with others, we watch how they handle all kinds of situations. They might not even have to say anything, because we're watching their attitude, behavior, and demeanor.

What does your attitude reflect in general? Do you see the same patterns in your parents or other people who influenced your formative years? The apostle Paul encourages us to have the same attitude of Jesus, and he later goes on to describe that attitude. Ultimately, he sums it up in one word: humility.

God, give me the grace to align my heart and my attitude with yours. Help me to be more like Jesus with my attitude today. Humble me and let others see an attitude of humility in me as well.

PARTNERSHIP

The LORD GOD said, "It is not good for the man to be alone.
I will make a helper suitable for him."
GENESIS 2:18 NIV

As followers of Jesus, we were never meant to do life alone. As men, it's important for us to have a partner, whether it be a spouse, a mother, a sibling, or just a friend, to help us out. God's creative intention was for partnership and community. He even models what relationship looks like through an expression of the Father, Son, and Holy Spirit.

Learn to first be in a partnership with God as you continue to trust him with your life. Then as you recognize the different partners you have been blessed with, take the opportunity to express your gratitude for their participation in your life. And don't be afraid to have the hard conversations about how you can support and encourage one another going forward. You were never meant to do this alone, and God will show you that you don't have to.

God, help me to realize that I was never meant to do life alone. May I trust in you and learn to be in even greater partnership with my "helper."

BRINGING PEACE

Let the peace of Christ rule in your hearts, since as members of one body you were called to peace. And be thankful.
COLOSSIANS 3:15 NIV

The people of Colossae were only familiar with a certain kind of peace when the apostle Paul wrote these words. They knew of a peace that was only accomplished through conquering war by Caesar and the Roman Empire. But Paul says let the peace of Christ be the ruler in your heart. This is a provocative statement, because most certainly the peace of Christ looked very different from the peace that was accomplished by Caesar. It looked like mercy, humility, love, and sacrifice, not dominating or conquering force.

Sometimes, as men, we think we'll make peace in our lives by asserting more authority and more power. But it's quite the opposite for followers of Jesus. The only way we bring peace is through peace. When it seems like there is chaos in your life, a natural reaction might be to puff up more, raise your voice more, and be more expressive with your actions. But try establishing a demeanor of peace before engaging in the situation. It will feel counterintuitive at first and may take time to get used to, but ultimately you'll be modeling the way of peace that Jesus desires for us.

God, grant me peace amid the chaos.

DOUBT

*The eleven disciples went to Galilee, to the mountain
where Jesus had told them to go. When they saw him,
they worshiped him; but some doubted.*
MATTHEW 28:16-17 NIV

This is, without a doubt, one of the greatest passages in
the New Testament. I like to imagine the disciples arriving at
the top of this mountain covered in dust, pushing each other,
making fun of one another, and giving the slowest members
of the group a hard time. When they get to the top, Jesus
is there. He is standing with them: present, powerful, and
purposeful. Matthew tells us that when they saw him, some
worshiped, but amazingly, some doubted. The word doubt
here means to "stand in two places." In other words, they
were there physically, but spiritually and emotionally they were
somewhere else.

Gathered in front of Jesus was the full spectrum of
discipleship. From passionate worshipers to those who
were troubled, doubting, and confused. What's absolutely
staggering is that Jesus doesn't make their current reality a
prerequisite for his Great Commission. In the very next verse,
he gives this group the instruction to go and change the
world. Clearly there's enough room on Team Jesus for those
who are struggling.

**Lord, I'm just like these disciples on any given day. I can
move from faith to doubt and back to faith again. Thank
you that you know that and you call me to your mission
regardless.**

ANGER

*Human anger does not produce
the righteousness God desires.*
JAMES 1:20 NLT

Can you remember a time when your mom or dad got angry with you? What did that feel like? Were they able to be angry while still being loving? Getting angry with people can be pretty common. Anger is not necessarily the issue; how we control our anger or manage it is what's imperative. James is not telling us, "Don't be angry." He's encouraging us to consider our anger and how it affects us as individuals and the people we love.

Think about a moment when you got angry with someone recently. Were you able to express your anger in love? You can tell someone that a particular situation made you upset; they need to know that. They also need to know why that situation made you upset. Then, take time to consider how anger can affect you and your relationships. Does your anger change the way you feel about the person you are angry with?

God, help me in my anger. Develop in me patience and self-control so I can still show love to others when I am angry.

ACTION

Don't just listen to God's word. You must do what it says.
Otherwise, you are only fooling yourselves.
JAMES 1:22 NLT

As you grow in your relationship with God, some of the natural desires that develop are prayer, reading Scripture, and joining together with a Christian community. When James spoke about doing "what it says," he was referring to a kind of action that results in justice: hope for the hopeless. Just a few verses later, he speaks of caring for the widows and orphans—the poor. Evidently, these two people groups were largely neglected, and often the prophets before Christ called out the people of God on their neglect. James seems to say that following Jesus looks like standing with the marginalized, the poor, and the broken, because faith without works is dead.

How can you model this kind of lifestyle? Maybe start out small by considering how you interact with a cashier or a restaurant server. How do you interact with people of different ethnic backgrounds or even the poor? You may find that others will begin to imitate your actions, so consider acting out justice.

God, give me your heart for broken people. Help me to consider ways that I can stand with them and care for them, because ultimately you cared for me.

LOVE DEEPLY

Above all, love each other deeply,
because love covers over a multitude of sins.
1 PETER 4:8 NIV

Sometimes hearing the words "Above all, love" over and over may sound like a broken record. It really is that simple, but it's also important to recognize the complexity of the final half of the verse: "covers over a multitude of sins." Peter is not trying to say the "sins" never took place or that we should somehow deny them. This is more of a proactive statement that if we love one another deeply and live in a rhythm of love, we may be less prone to participating in the brokenness of sin.

Sin is still real and still present, but love is far more powerful. It's also a reactive statement in that love can heal sin. It doesn't take away from the fact that the sin occurred, but love has the power to heal and restore. How might this be expressed in your life? You are going to make mistakes, there's no denying that. But if you continuously move toward love, you will experience healing and restoration.

God, show me love today, and help me to show others love as well.

HOSPITALITY

*Cheerfully share your home with those
who need a meal or a place to stay.*
1 PETER 4:9 NLT

In ancient Eastern culture, hospitality was paramount. To say that it would be an honor to have someone over for dinner would be an understatement. In Western culture, however, we seem to be always on the go. We don't usually stop to have a meal for hours at a time with guests, instead frequenting the drive-through on our way to the next event. Hospitality may be a dying art, but let's revive it.

It's important for us to be intentional when we interact with guests who come to our homes no matter how nice our homes are, no matter how great the meal is, and no matter how long they stay. For followers of Jesus, there is something sacred about sharing a meal together in a home with another family. When you break bread and talk about life and faith and whatever else comes up, it's a holy moment. Make room for more of those moments. Interestingly, in the book of Revelation, Jesus makes mention of knocking at a door and coming in to share a meal. Perhaps there's something to that.

God, help me to be open and proactive in inviting people into my home.

HUMILITY OR TRUST

If you bow low in God's awesome presence, he will eventually exalt you as you leave the timing in his hands. Pour out all your worries and stress upon him and leave them there, for he always tenderly cares for you.

1 PETER 5:6-7 TPT

In American culture, it seems like everyone wants to be the best and get to the top. In fact, we encourage it. It's in our DNA to succeed, and it's the air we breathe. And getting to the top is often in conflict with humility and trust; those character traits are seen as weak or passive.

As followers of Jesus, however, humbling one's self is the start of true character and integrity. As men, we can struggle with this. Often, we want to display to others that we have it all together, because if we show any weakness, then they might not trust us or feel secure with us. But we follow a God who, in Jesus, submitted himself to death on a cross because of his humility. Let's trust that our humility will lead to greater trust in God, and in the meantime rid ourselves of the insecurity of being honest about our fears and anxieties. We don't have to impress God—good thing!

God, I admit that I cannot do this on my own. I need you. I am not invincible. Fill me with trust.

WORLDLINESS

Do not love this world nor the things it offers you,
for when you love the world,
you do not have the love of the Father in you.
1 JOHN 2:15 NLT

There is so much about our world that is enticing, and it should be. We were created in the image of God, so we're creative beings. Humankind has come up with some truly unique creations. However, there are also certain worldly creations that distract us from God. In a lot of ways, they reflect the opposite of the character that God wants to produce within us. There's no need for a list of these; you know the things in your life that lead you away from God.

Instead, think about the love of God. What would it look like for you to be so filled with the love of God that you wouldn't have enough room in your heart for the things of this world? The goal isn't to escape anything; that just produces fear and separation. The goal is to be confronted with the challenges of the world and not be phased by them (or at least controlled by them). What can you do today to increase God's love in your life?

God, prepare my heart to be secure in you. Help me to resist the temptations of the world that lead me away from you.

PAIN AND JOY

*"He will wipe every tear from their eyes,
and there will be no more death or sorrow or crying or pain.
All these things are gone forever."*
REVELATION 21:4 NLT

As followers of Jesus, it's important for us to live with hope no matter our circumstances. The hope we have in Jesus leads to something like what John wrote about in Revelation. He saw an image of no more sadness, just pure joy. The question is, how do we start living in that reality right now? And how do we encourage others to understand that as well?

At a fairly young age, most kids get the concept of joy and pain; but as we get older, we tend to complicate these things. Try imagining what it could look like to have a world where there's no more pain, suffering, or sadness. Describe what true joy looks like to you. It could be something serious or something silly. The idea is to get in the habit of thinking futuristically, imagining a future with nothing but joy and then beginning to live in that future right now. This is what hope in Jesus can look like. Get creative!

God, develop a greater hope within me to see your kingdom come and your will be done on earth now as it is in heaven. Help me to imagine a world without pain.

NEWNESS

The one sitting on the throne said, "Look, I am making everything new!" And then he said to me, "Write this down, for what I tell you is trustworthy and true."
REVELATION 21:5 NLT

We all like new things. New clothes, new gadgets, new phones, new cars, it doesn't matter what it is as long as it's brand-new. And we like to be able to provide these things for ourselves and others in our life.

There's a different kind of newness that comes with being a follower of Jesus. Each day seems like a new opportunity to grow in our faith, to encounter someone in need of the love of God, or to simply breathe another breath of air. God promises to make us new in this life, and even in the end, there is a vision that God will make all things new. It's almost as if Jesus takes every broken thing and restores it, repurposes it, or revitalizes it. Where do you need newness in your life? What new thing can you do to show your love for others today? Consider the newness of each day; it's another opportunity to show the people in your life how special they really are.

God, remind me that each new day is a blessing. No matter what challenges I face, help me to never forget the gift of life.

SMALL BEGINNINGS

"Do not despise these small beginnings,
for the LORD rejoices to see the work begin,
to see the plumb line in Zerubbabel's hand."
ZECHARIAH 4:10 NLT

Grand visions are just that. Grand. Big. But each of them begins with the smallest of steps. The rebuilding of the Lord's temple after the people returned from Babylon was no different. Before the ornate interior was the roof. Before the roof, the walls. Before the walls was the floor. Before the floor was the foundation. And that foundation? It began with a single brick set into the ground.

According to Zechariah, it was Zerubbabel who laid that very first brick of the foundation and it would be Zerubbabel who would set the final stone. A single brick is a small thing. A small beginning. A very crucial beginning. Life is a lot like that. As men, we often have grand goals for ourselves, but we don't know where or how to begin. Start with a small goal, then keep building.

God, you do not despise the small things. Often, I feel like a small brick in a great wall. But you find joy in those small beginnings because without them there is no completion. Help me to be willing to take the small steps.

FAVORITES

Now Israel [Jacob] loved Joseph
more than all of his children.
GENESIS 37:3 NKJV

Playing favorites was nothing new to the family of Jacob. His own mother, Rebekah, preferred him over his brother, Esau, and together they had tricked Isaac into giving Jacob the birthright meant for Esau. And when Jacob played favorites with Joseph, he unknowingly set his son on a collision course with pride and arrogance, which caused many problems with his older brothers.

Each person has different gifts and talents, and these were given by God. As men, we may be tempted to look upon some of those gifts with greater favor than others, but when we do this, we can transfer this favor to certain people in our lives, creating bad feelings among friends and family members and resentment toward us. As men, let's pay close attention to the way we show love to those closest to us, according to who God made them to be.

Father, you do not play favorites. You reveal your grace to all through the sacrifice of your Son, Jesus Christ. And, while you give different gifts and measures of grace, your love for each of us is total, complete, and perfect. Help me to love people in this same way.

LISTEN

Hear O Israel:
the LORD our God,
the LORD is one.
DEUTERONOMY 6:4 NIV

The verse above is the beginning of the daily Jewish prayer, commonly called the Shema, which is Hebrew for "listen." It sets the tone for the rest of the prayer because it orients the person praying to whom he is praying to. It is God's people, Israel, who must listen as God is described—his name, nature, and character.

It is we who must listen, because we are surrounded by gods that "are not gods" (Jeremiah 16:20). We must call others to hear about "the Lord our God," the one and only Lord and Deliverer, so they will not be confused. Men who do this will be speaking honestly, clearly, and consistently about the who of God. We can only do this proclaiming when we know him personally.

Father, I'm here to hear about you. The only God. The one true God. My God. You are clear and direct with me; please give me that same clarity when calling others to hear about you.

TOTAL LOVE

*Love the LORD your God with all your heart
and with all your soul and with all your strength.*
DEUTERONOMY 6:5 NIV

Once we have acknowledged the who of God (our God, one God), a response is required. An action. The right response is to love God with all of who we are, because love is a verb. This love is full and complete—all of our heart, all of our soul, and all of our strength.

Men have the daily opportunity to not only love the Lord totally but to also show this same love to others, not as just an act toward them but also as a demonstration of love toward God. They experience this heart love when they see our emotion, our soul love when they see our sincerity, and our strength love when they see us exert energy for them. People in our lives learn about total devotion to God from us, so let's love them well!

God, please show me the areas in my life where my active love for you falls short of your command. Is my heart in it? Do I feel emotional love for you? Does my love for you indicate effort? Am I striving to love you with all of me? Thank you for being devoted to me.

COMMIT

You must commit yourselves wholeheartedly to these commands that I am giving you today.
DEUTERONOMY 6:6 NLT

We live in an overcommitted age, and so much of what we do requires total commitment. Our electronic devices make us available 24/7. The activities that we participate in take more time, money, and effort than ever before. As soon as one activity ends, another begins. Sometimes it seems like we can barely keep up!

God also has a requirement, not to an activity or availability, but to his commands. We need to commit to them, to follow and obey them. As men, the way we obey God's commands reveals much about our commitment to him. Being committed means more than just knowing the commands; we also need to follow them and understand that they keep us focused on him and that they protect us. When you show your total commitment to God's commands to those around you, you show them where your heart is.

God, open my heart to your commands. Allow me not just to learn them but to be committed to them and to see them as a gift to me that keeps me in line with your will and protects me from hardship and evil.

REPEAT

Repeat them again and again to your children. Talk about them when you are at home and when you are on the road, when you are going to bed and when you are getting up.
DEUTERONOMY 6:7 NLT

We learn best by repetition. We learn best by repetition. We learn best by repetition. (No, that is not a typo!) We study words to learn to spell. Playing a musical instrument is simple muscle memory. We drive the same route every day so we know how to time it right to hit nothing but green lights. And many of us have spent hours shooting free throws.

The commands of God are no different. We read the Scriptures not just for a way to live, but to know and understand the way of Jesus. We learn them and then talk about them, always. We become so familiar with God's Word that it overflows out of us, and we talk about it with people every chance we get. We make the most of every moment because passing on the faith is our primary task. When we drive. When we lie down. When we rise. Always.

Father, help me to fall so in love with your Word that it overflows and absolutely infects every conversation with friends and family. I want to study and learn your commands again and again so they are always on my mind.

PUT ON

*Tie them to your hands and wear them
on your foreheads as reminders.*
DEUTERONOMY 6:8 NLT

Men love to do. We feel most comfortable when we are taking action, whether at play, at home, or at work. We fear being seen by others as lazy. At times, we do so much that we're simply busy as opposed to actually accomplishing something of value. But when we tie God's commands to our hands, we're acting upon them. We go beyond understanding and put them into practice. We actually serve others; we do something. Wearing these commands on our head happens when we're transparent about whom we serve and why we do what we do. We talk about Jesus and are unafraid to share the motivation for our actions. These things are not busy work, but incredibly important and valuable.

When we wear God's commands, people get to see us live out what we say we believe. When we act upon those beliefs, they learn that what we believe is more than something we simply intellectually assent to. Rather, it is who we are.

Lord, as I listen to, love, commit to, and repeat your commands, let me act upon them. Daily I meet people in need of you, not just your words, but you. As James says, my deeds reveal my faith. Let them be bold!

WRITE

*Write them on the doorposts of your house
and on your gates.*
DEUTERONOMY 6:9 NLT

Take a moment and look at the clothes you're wearing. Chances are there's a brand label clearly visible for all to see. We're walking advertisements, and we provide this service free of charge. In fact, we pay the brand. Perhaps we simply like the style or the fit, but more likely the brand means something to us.

When we write God's commands on our doorposts and gates, we are advertising him. And he has paid us to do this. First Corinthians 6:20 tells us that we have been bought for a price: his Son, Jesus Christ. By accepting this, we put him on display; he is our brand, and we belong to him, not in the form of a catchy saying, but in the form of our actions of love, mercy, and grace. This begins at home as we show these things to our friends and family. Put Christ on display!

God, as I dress today, help me to look at each label on my clothing and ask myself what those labels and logos say about the brand. Then, give me the presence of mind to ask how my thoughts, words, and deeds reveal you to all those I'll meet today.

BE STRONG

"Be strong and courageous,
for you must go with this people into the land
that the LORD swore to their ancestors to give them."

DEUTERONOMY 31:7 NIV

The heart of God is one of strength and courage. While we know this for many reasons, it is most obvious through his Son, Jesus. God didn't simply give his people a set of rules and regulations to follow; he entered into their world, going with his people into the activities of their lives. He struggled, faced temptation, and knew hunger and thirst. He was tired. He worked. He laughed. He confronted sin and selfish attitudes. And he is still with us today.

In the same way, a man who leads enters the world of those around him. He encourages them. Works and labors with them. Instructs them from a close proximity. This requires strength and courage because it seems easier just to give orders and make rules. A good leader, just like Christ, is close to those he leads and shares in their struggles.

Lord, I want to be strong and courageous! I want to follow the example of Jesus, entering into the lives of those I lead. I want to know their experiences, their hurts, and their successes. I want to know them deeply. I want them to know that I am with them.

WONDERFULLY MADE

I praise you because I am fearfully
and wonderfully made:
your works are wonderful,
I know that full well.
PSALM 139:14 NIV

It's easy for us to think about and apply this verse to ourselves as individuals, and it's easy for us to think about and apply these verses to others. Until... promises aren't kept. Someone needs another favor. That certain friend cancels, yet again. Debts aren't repaid. Another Saturday is consumed by helping a friend move.

People can require a lot of us. Even in these moments, God's truth rings out: humans are fearfully and wonderfully made.

Father, you made each person in your very image. In that image you set purpose and intentionality. No details were left to chance. Each and every aspect of those you have brought into my life brings you glory and reveals something about yourself. I love the joyous moments, and it's so easy to see you in them. But life is also filled with challenges and unexpected, and sometimes disappointing, actions. You are there too. Let me see you then.

GENTLENESS

A soft answer turns away wrath,
but a harsh word stirs up anger.
PROVERBS 15:1 NIV

Gentleness is a fruit of the Spirit, an evidence that God is at work in us as the Holy Spirit takes residency in our heart. Because of this, the way we speak to people can reveal the degree to which the Holy Spirit influences and impacts our lives.

Sometimes, it is those who are closest to us who can drive us crazy the most. We all have that certain friend or family member who requires an extra measure of grace. This can try our patience, but the way we respond to them will often be directly proportional to the level of grace we have received from the Holy Spirit. And when it comes to grace, God give freely, so we should do the same. Gentleness requires that we be present in the moment, remembering that our words are powerful and that gentle ones are best.

Lord, I remember many harsh words said to me in response to something I'd said or done. Frequently, that led to escalation and greater misunderstanding, then harder feelings, and more harsh words. Help me to reflect on those moments and give me the desire to respond in ways that honor you.

NOVEMBER

That's why I take pleasure in my
weaknesses, and in the insults,
hardships, persecutions, and
troubles that I suffer for Christ. For
when I am weak, then I am strong.

2 CORINTHIANS 12:10 NLT

BE REAL

*I remember your genuine faith, for you share the faith that first
filled your grandmother Lois and your mother, Eunice. And I
know that same faith continues strong in you.*

2 TIMOTHY 1:5 NLT

The little word genuine that the apostle Paul uses here is
a term that means real, or without hypocrisy. Really, it means
that there's an alignment between who you say you are and
who you are. It's a challenge toward authenticity, toward being
straight and unwavering. Amazing, awesome, and epic seem
like little hills against the mountain of genuine faith.

Genuine faith lived out in the context of friends and family
gives hope, something to admire, and something to follow.
Timothy learned this from both his mother and grandmother!
Do you love a challenge, and do your loved ones need you to
be a mountain climber? Start climbing today!

**God, help me straighten out the crooked ways within me.
Make me one person, inside and out, and allow the people
in my life to catch a glimpse of a genuine faith, a real
relationship between Jesus and me.**

BE PASSIONATE

I remind you to rekindle the gift of God
that is within you through the laying on of my hands.
2 TIMOTHY 1:6 NRSV

The apostle Paul adopted some young men into his leadership team and treated them as his family. One of these was Timothy, who struggled with the demands of leadership. In 2 Timothy 1:6, we get a behind-the-scenes glimpse of a father motivating a son to be all he can be. Paul used the metaphor of a fire, one that is lit but barely, like a summer campfire the next morning. Some of the wood has aglow. With a little work, it could be a raging fire again. Paul told Timothy that it was time to restoke the fires of his heart. This was really a moment of reflection for the young pastor. He was being asked, "Is there still a love for Jesus in your heart, like there once was?" Paul was saying, "I've seen passionate faith in you. It's time to let the fire burn again."

Men, take some time to remember when you were passionate for Christ. Remember when he had captured your affections and the good news about Jesus was everything to you, and when the fire raged as your heart was set on Jesus Christ. Let's ask God to help us rediscover a passionate faith.

God, thank you for kindling my heart with power, love, and self-control. Now I ask you to ignite the fire, let the fresh wind of your Spirit catch the flame, and let my heart rage for you once more.

BE BRAVE

God gave us a spirit not of fear
but of power and love and self-control.
2 TIMOTHY 1:7 ESV

We can have so many fear-filled moments as men. Fear for the uncertainty of our futures, fear of the mounting responsibilities that get added to our lists daily, and fear that those we love will reject us or forget us, or even hate us. Life can be a fear-filled space. Acknowledge the fear, but don't let it stop your moving forward.

Instead, recognize that God lives inside you and that the tools he has equipped you with—power, love, and self-control—are greater than fear. When fear fills your heart and your knees tremble, it's time to go forward anyway, remembering that God is with you and in you.

God, fill me with courage, risk taking, and adventure, and let your power, love, and self-control overcome my fears. Greater is he that is in me than he that is in the world.

BE LOYAL

Join with me in suffering, like a good soldier of Christ Jesus.
No one serving as a soldier gets entangled in civilian affairs,
but rather tries to please his commanding officer.
2 TIMOTHY 2:3-4 NIV

When the apostle Paul challenged his young spiritual son Timothy to be a military man, he was not asking him to take up arms, join the army, and learn how to fight. He was challenging him to be loyal. In those years, many of the soldiers fighting on behalf of the Roman Empire were mercenaries. In fact, whole legions were financed and supported to go to war on behalf of one nation or another. History tells of entire armies switching sides because they got a better cash deal.

As men, leaders, and believers, we have already pledged our allegiance to King Jesus. This Scripture is encouraging us to remain loyal. Don't get distracted by what seems like a better deal. There is no better deal. You're already on the winning team. Victory is ours through Christ Jesus. Death is defeated, sin is under our feet, and glory waits for those who please the commanding officer. Don't get distracted. Bow your knee. Receive your orders. Be obedient.

King Jesus, I humble myself before your leadership. As my commander in chief, I give you your rightful place as Lord and King. Help me to remain loyal to you and your call.

BE UNDIVIDED

Athletes cannot win the prize
unless they follow the rules.
2 TIMOTHY 2:5 NLT

The Rio Olympics were marred by allegations of cheating and drug abuse by the Russian Athletics Federation. When Russian athletes competed, they were greeted by taunts and boos from the crowd. Cheating in sports is not a new thing. From the earliest documented history of the Olympic Games, we can track the problem of athletes not competing according to the rules. Records show details of athletes caught using bribery, match fixing, and even food poisoning to gain an edge over their opponents.

The entrance to the ancient stadium in Greece was lined with golden statues of Zeus and other gods. These statues were placed there not as a tribute to the gods but to remind athletes not to cheat. If caught cheating, the athlete would have to take a public flogging followed by paying the hefty bill for one of these statues to be erected in their honor as a cheat. At the bottom of the statue their name would be immortalized, known forever as one who didn't compete according to the rules. In a culture where getting ahead is culturally acceptable, to be an athlete—a true athlete—you must be a man of integrity, living in a state of being whole and undivided. In other words, you are the same person off the track as you are on it.

God, help me be undivided. Make me a man of integrity.
Show me how I can grow, and equip me for the race of faith.

GET YOUR HANDS DIRTY

*Hardworking farmers should be the first
to enjoy the fruit of their labor.*
2 TIMOTHY 2:6 NLT

The apostle Paul loved to communicate by painting pictures with words. As a spiritual dad to a young man learning to become a pastor, he liked to make his teaching memorable and meaningful. A life of faith and leadership is like being a soldier, an athlete, and a farmer. A soldier's life is marked by a quest for glory. An athlete is chasing the dream of gold, fame, and honor. The farmer's journey, however, is different. There is no honor and no glory in the field. There is just mud, sweat, and tears. But after lots of hard work, in the right time and in the right season, there is a harvest and the farmer gets to enjoy it first.

Being a man is messy business. We find ourselves with dirty hands from the toil and strife of life. We are working in the muck and yuck of a broken world. There are seasons when it is all sweat and tears. The hardworking farmer knows that the harvest is coming, and he is close enough to the action to be able to appreciate it first. Don't run away from the hard work of being a man. Roll your sleeves up and get mucked in!

God, give me a farmer's heart. Help me understand what season I am in and to trust you that the harvest is coming.

GET READY

You should know this, Timothy,
that in the last days there will be very difficult times.
2 TIMOTHY 3:1 NLT

When the apostle Paul wrote about difficult times in the last days, he was talking about the very times we find ourselves living in now. The word difficult comes from a term that was used to describe a wild animal on a rampage or a ship at sea during a dangerous storm. In other words, there will be people and circumstances that come against you. Following Jesus well involves navigating through a complex maze of relationships and circumstances, none of which are guaranteed with comfort or safety. These were important words from Paul to his true son in the faith. It was important that he equipped Timothy for the real world.

The same is true of our calling as men. It's an adventure of action-packed challenges, ups and downs, real relationships with conflict and healing, and real circumstances: some good some bad. It is not only our job as men to navigate these experiences, but it is also our calling to equip others to do the same. Paul was writing from a dungeon prison in Rome, awaiting his execution, alone and struggling and missing Timothy. This is a good word to us as men. Let us use our life experiences to prepare and equip others for theirs.

Heavenly Father, give me the wisdom to see opportunities when my journey can equip others for theirs. Give me courage to face the storms of life and to show my friends and family how to trust you in the midst of them.

BE FOCUSED

People will be lovers of themselves, lovers of money,
boasters, arrogant, abusive, disobedient to their parents,
ungrateful, unholy.
2 TIMOTHY 3:2 NRSV

"Money makes the world go around," as the old adage says. While it is true that money is needed to provide our basic needs, the Bible warns us that the love of money is the first step toward all kinds of sin (1 Timothy 6:10). So, which is it?

As men, we have a strong drive to provide for our needs and the needs of others. This is a natural desire as there is nothing inherently wrong with money. However, problems begin to arise when we focus on the money itself, and not the good that we can do with it. After all, money is meant to serve us, and we serve the Lord. What are some ways you can refocus your priorities to ensure that a love for money hasn't ensnared your heart?

God, help me to have a biblical view of money, and to see the riches you have provided as a blessing. May I use your blessing to bless others.

KEEP GOING

*Continue in what you have learned and have firmly believed,
knowing from whom you learned it.*
2 TIMOTHY 3:14 ESV

When it comes to being a man, you're smashing it out of the park! All the time you've invested in your friends and family, all the time and dedication spent on your career, and all the time devoted on your knees praying, and seeking the presence of the Lord. Be encouraged today. You're doing a great work. Being a man feels like a boxing match sometimes. But whatever you do, don't give up.

Young Timothy, a pastor and leader in a New Testament church, wanted to quit. His calling was a tough one. But these words of wisdom were given to him from his spiritual father: "You know who you are. You know what you are about, you know what I am about. Now take a deep breath and let's get back into the fight." You know who you are. You have been called by God, and you know what you are about. So refocus on your values and remember what is important. Get back in the fight today.

God, speak to my identity today and use that to call me back into the game. Help me keep going. I trust you. Lead me.

THE WORD

All scripture is inspired by God and is useful for teaching,
for reproof, for correction, and for training in righteousness.
2 TIMOTHY 3:16 NRSV

There aren't many men who feel adequately equipped for their calling. We are growing, we are learning, and we are being transformed, but truthfully we still feel the weight of life as a man, and it is heavy! It's a serious business. In the middle of all the changes, the ongoing transformation, the chaos of relationships, and the growing pains of life, Paul reminds young Timothy of two things that never change: God's Word and his gift of salvation through Jesus Christ. Whatever your journey is throwing at you, learn to hold on tight to these two immovable objects.

Allow God's Word to be your daily guide. Let it shape you and strengthen you for your calling to manhood. Hold fast to the amazing gift of your salvation. You are no longer your own, but your life is hidden with Christ. You are secure in him. No matter what comes your way today, choose to listen to his Word and cling to the one who is holding tight to you.

God, let your holy Word guide my day, equipping me to be a great and godly man, because of Christ Jesus.

THE MAIN THING

Preach the word of God.
Be prepared, whether the time is favorable or not.
Patiently correct, rebuke, and encourage your people
with good teaching.

2 TIMOTHY 4:2 NLT

Every man is telling a story. As we live our lives, manage our resources, and leave our relational footprint in the community, we're all making a noise, leaving a mark. You are no different. What story are you telling your world?

In the verse above, Paul was teaching Timothy about the importance of connecting our story to God's story and letting the noise we make be the noise God is making. This young pastor was being encouraged to keep the main thing the main thing. He was being encouraged to be open and ready to be used by God. Finally, he was being reminded to take his learning and use it to build up those around him. How can you connect God's Word to your story today? How can God use you to see his story extended into your world? How can you take his Word and use it to encourage your friends and family, to build them up and connect them to God's story?

God, make me a man of your Word. When I read it, let it read me. Make your Word the living Word for me, that I can learn your ways and help others discover them.

DON'T FOLLOW THE CROWD

The time is coming when people will not put up with sound doctrine, but having itching ears, they will accumulate for themselves teachers to suit their own desires, and will turn away from listening to the truth and wander away to myths.

2 TIMOTHY 4:3-4 NRSV

Dads love to see their kids stand out. They get so excited when they score a goal in soccer, get an assist in hockey, or nail the lead role in the school play. They love to see their kids shine bright and are thrilled when they step out of the ordinary into the extraordinary. In short, they love it when their kids go against the flow. The apostle Paul was forecasting a time in the future when his young son Timothy would be under serious pressure to conform to the overwhelming flow of his culture. The pressure to run with the pack would be so great, and the bright light of Timothy's calling would be extinguished.

Just like a good coach in the locker room, Paul looks his quarterback in the eye and inspires him to get out onto the field and get the win. Timothy is challenged to get his helmet on and get to work. It's his time to shine. What a great word to us. The pressure is on and the culture is squeezing, but we were made for so much more. You were made for so much more.

Father, thank you for making me unique, special, and specific in my calling. Help me to shine for you today.

GET THE JOB DONE

Work at telling others the Good News,
and fully carry out the ministry God has given you.
2 TIMOTHY 4:5 NLT

Men love to be practical. We love to see our team mobilized, active, and participating in the practical realities of life, whether it be in sports, work, or our families. As Jesus followers, we are called to do the same. When the apostle Paul wrote to his son Timothy encouraging him to keep the message alive, he was telling him it's time to get practical. He wasn't talking about preaching; we know that because just a couple of verses previously, he instructed the young pastor to preach the word (verse 2).

No, in this particular Scripture we're being challenged as believers to make sure our message has hands and feet. Just as Jesus came to serve and demonstrate the good news, we are being asked to do the same. So today look for practical, tangible ways to express the message that we proclaim. Show those around you that we're not just a people with a book; we are a people with a mission! Let's get the job done!

God, you are awesome. Thank you that we don't all need to be preachers. Show me practical and helpful ways today that I can lovingly demonstrate the kingdom of God to my world.

EYES ON THE PRIZE

I have fought the good fight, I have finished the race, I have kept the faith. Now there is in store for me the crown of righteousness, which the Lord, the righteous Judge, will award to me on that day—and not only to me, but also to all who have longed for his appearing.

2 TIMOTHY 4:7-8 NIV

There probably isn't a more manly verse in Scripture than 2 Timothy 4:7-8. The apostle Paul considers his life to have been a wrestling match. There are many days like that for us too. Some days there is actual wrestling, when a friend playfully tries to strong-arm us to the floor. Some days the wrestling is on a deep, spiritual, and transformational level. It is rough, gritty, and dirty. But we were made to be in the fight.

Our journey is also likened to a long-distance race. Perhaps you're a distance runner and so you know well how to strategize, organize your energy, and dig deep for that inner resolve to press on to the finish line. Listen up, men, we are fitter and stronger than we realize. We were made for the fight, and we were designed for the race. The key to being successful is keeping your eye on the prize and your ears attuned to the coach. The crown of righteousness awaits, and your coach, King Jesus, is cheering you on, shouting instructions and sharing his experience. Don't stop fighting and don't stop running.

King Jesus, fill me with courage to fight the good fight, and energize my soul to run hard today. Help me fix my eyes on the prize.

BROTHERHOOD

The Lord stood at my side and gave me strength,
so that through me the message might be fully proclaimed.
2 TIMOTHY 4:17 NIV

In ancient warfare, there was nothing more important than the man who stood at your side. When the Roman troops prepared to defend themselves against the arrows flying through the air, they formed a tight wall and each soldier's shield covered the man to his right. You were completely dependent upon the man on your left side; he was your shield and defender.

It's time to get some good men around us. This fight of faith is too big, too dangerous, and too scary to go alone into battle. Yes, we want the Lord at our side, but part of how he designed discipleship is that we stand side by side with our brothers. They take care of us and we take care of them. We were not made to do this alone. Who is standing at your side, covering you with his shield, fighting for you, encouraging you, and covering your back? If you know, then praise God for that man or those men. If you don't know who that is, it's time to ask God to bring these men into your life.

God, help me to reach out to other men today. I want to stand side by side with other men who are fighting the good fight of faith. Connect me to men of courage, honor, and integrity.

EVERYTHING YOU NEED

The Lord be with your spirit.
Grace be with you all.
2 TIMOTHY 4:22 NIV

Here goes another crazy day in the life of a man. Driving, working, driving more, friends, family, church, and sports. Let's be real for a moment. It's a lot. It's nonstop. It's hard. It's a wrestling match. It's a long-distance race. Life can be so busy! The apostle Paul, as he signed off from a life of ministry, had one final word for his young son spiritual Timothy. This rookie pastor, overwhelmed by his calling, his weakness, and his limitations, must have been taking a deep breath as the aging apostle handed him the leadership of the gospel movement. In the last sentence of his final letter, Paul tells Timothy that everything he needs for all that's ahead is found in two things: God's presence and God's grace.

Men, let's learn to lean in to these important things today. God is with us, and his grace is for us. Our resources are limited, but his are not. Our emotional capacity is small and our ability to fight temptation and sin is little, but his grace is great. It is strong. It is enough. Your challenge today is to remind yourself of the abiding, unrelenting presence of Jesus and to accept his grace into your life.

God, help me to take a deep breath. Instead of being stressed and overwhelmed, may I realize that you are with me, you are in me, and your grace is over me.

THE AMAZING NEWS

"The time has come," he said.
"The kingdom of God has come near.
Repent and believe the good news!"
MARK 1:15 NIV

God is near. Really near. He's just a decision away. Did you ever color on the walls when you were a kid, but when it came time to clean it off you just weren't strong enough to get the job done? Perhaps with tears in your eyes you would look up and say, "Daddy, help."

Repentance is a beautiful gift. It's the simple, Spirit-led moment of realizing we don't have the capacity to wash the walls of our lives. Then, by God's amazing grace, we simply turn around, and when we do, we find that God is near. The King and his kingdom are at hand. Our Daddy help has arrived.

God, I can't believe you're so close. I'm sorry for always trying to do everything in my own strength. Forgive me and let your kingdom power come into my life.

NEW THINGS

As he walked along, he saw Levi son of Alphaeus sitting at the tax collector's booth. "Follow me," Jesus told him, and Levi got up and followed him.

MARK 2:14 NIV

Jesus called Levi to be a disciple, even though nobody liked, trusted, or communed with tax collectors, such as Levi. It's pretty amazing that someone so despised would be so welcomed into a religious community. There's a deeper story here though. Levi is identified as the son of Alphaeus. In all likelihood, Levi was a tax collector because that was the family business. Levi was who he was because his father was who he was. Then Jesus entered his story, called this publican, and invited him into a different story. Levi accepted and was never again identified as the son of Alphaeus. This is incredibly freeing news, but it's also deeply challenging.

First, we men don't need to be defined by who our fathers were or how they raised us. Second, we must face the reality of our lives and the impact we have on those closest to us. We desperately need Jesus to call us into a new story and to equip us to simply follow him.

Lord Jesus, thank you for your beautiful call to follow you. I want to live in your story today. Thank you that I am not defined by my past and that your call is a call into new things.

WELCOME TO THE FAMILY

*"Whoever does God's will
is my brother and sister and mother."*
MARK 3:35 NIV

Every family has issues, including Jesus'. Ponder that for a moment and maybe even quietly enjoy the deep encouragement that this simple thought from Scripture gives us. Jesus, the Son of God, had a dysfunctional family. Not everything was Instagram perfect. Jesus had been busy in his ministry, training his disciples, teaching about his kingdom, and healing the sick. Crowds were following him, and everyone was getting excited. Well, everyone except for Jesus' own family. Their response was pretty shocking: "When his family heard about this, they went to take charge of him, for they said, 'He is out of his mind'" (Mark 3:21). After the dust had settled, Jesus explained to his followers that in his movement, his emerging kingdom, community, family, and belonging were being redefined.

To be in Jesus' family, the priority must be to discover and do the will of God. As men, it's critical that we remember how family works in the kingdom. We need to ensure we're helping the people in our lives to first discover and second to do the will of God. Sometimes this might mean setting our plans, our leadership, and our understanding out of the way.

Lord, thank you for my friends and family. They are a gift, and I want to honor that. Help me, as a man, to passionately pursue your will, and give me the courage to help others do the same.

JESUS, MESSIAH

"Why are you so afraid?
Do you still have no faith?"
MARK 4:40 NIV

The people of Israel had a love-hate relationship with water. They had been delivered through the Red Sea during their Exodus, but their fear of the depths was still hanging over from Noah's flood. As they waited for their promised Messiah to arrive, a man named Isaiah foretold of his coming and his relationship to water: "When you pass through the waters, I will be with you; and when you pass through the rivers, they will not sweep over you" (Isaiah 43:2).

When Jesus was in the back of the boat after calming the storm and rebuking the disciples, he was really taking them back to Isaiah's promises about their deliverer. He was essentially saying, "Do you still not get it? I am the Promised One, and the Promised One can take care of a little storm on the sea." The disciples needed to connect the promises in the Word to the Promised One who was the Word. Men, let's take Jesus at his word. We need not fear any storm. He will be with us.

Lord God, thank you for sending your Messiah, King Jesus. Take my fears from the storms in my life and make your redeeming presence real to me today.

STORYTELLING

Jesus did not let him, but said, "Go home to your own people and tell them how much the Lord has done for you, and how he has had mercy on you."

MARK 5:19 NIV

Storytelling has always been the primary vehicle of transferring faith from one generation to the next. But in our times, it has become a lost art. Too often parents or grandparents fail to help their kids connect their lives to the good news about Jesus. This is actually a movement away from the very plan God showed his people in Scripture. The psalmist explains, "We will tell the next generation the praiseworthy deeds of the Lord, about his power and his mighty wonders" (Psalm 78:4). It is our responsibility to tell stories of faith to the next generation.

You don't have to be a parent or grandparent to participate. You also don't have to be a Bible school graduate or an ordained minister. You just need to discover your own story again. Take some time today to tell your loved ones about some of the amazing things that God has done in your life.

Lord, you are amazing. Thank you for the many ways you have changed my life. Give me a renewed passion for telling stories to the next generation: stories of hope, stories of provision, and stories of mission.

SENT

Calling the Twelve to him, he began to send them out two by two and gave them authority over impure spirits.
MARK 6:7 NIV

What a momentous occasion for these rag-tag teenage Jesus followers. Most of them were blue-collar workers, semiskilled in religious studies, and marred by negative cultural legacy. They were from Galilee, second-class citizens at best. Completely and utterly unqualified for the task ahead of them. Inexperienced, uneducated, and immature. The amazing thing about the generosity of God is that he doesn't just invite us to join him in his work; he also generously supplies all we need to live on a mission with him. For the disciples, he practically supplied teammates to journey with, to pray with, and to support and care for. He also spiritually provided the ability to get the job done. A certain set of tools are needed for kingdom building, and the King generously supplies them.

You have a massive calling on your life. Remember that you are inexperienced, you are a work in progress, and you are completely unqualified. The great news is that when the King calls, the King supplies. All you need today can be found in him. So ask God to show you his generosity today. You are called, and so you will be equipped.

Lord, replace my doubt, my fear, and my feelings of inadequacy with a deep sense of call, a confidence in my being sent by you. I look to you to supply all the resources I need today to get the job done.

FEAR NOT

"Fear not, for I am with you; be not dismayed, for I am your God. I will strengthen you, yes, I will help you, I will uphold you with My righteous right hand."

ISAIAH 41:10 NKJV

When you find yourself facing fear (fear of the future, fear of not being able to provide, fear of failure), remind yourself that you are not alone. God has promised that he is with you and that he will offer the strength you need. That he will uphold you and protect you. You can take shelter in his presence.

Just as a child runs to his daddy when he is fearful, run to God in your fear. He will wrap his arms around you and remind you of his perfect, powerful, and unwavering presence.

God, help me to be willing to come to you with my fears. Thank you that you have promised to be a shelter for me. Help me to find comfort, encouragement, and strength through resting in your presence.

GIVING THANKS

Whatever you do or say, do it as a representative of the Lord Jesus, giving thanks through him to God the Father.
COLOSSIANS 3:17 NLT

Sometimes the point of Christianity gets relegated to going to church, saying a prayer before a meal, and maybe reading the Bible from time to time. Those are all great and should be elements of one's faith, but according to the verse above, our whole selves are to reflect a picture of what Jesus is actually like. And everything we do and say should lead toward gratitude.

This seems like an impossible task, but there is actually a science to this. As humans practice being thankful in their mind and in their speech, it actually rewires pathways in their brain in a way that trains them to live their whole lives through a lens of gratitude. Consider keeping a journal of thankfulness or verbally practicing gratitude one or two times per day with the people in your life and see if it changes anything within you. You may be the person in their lives who can be the best picture of Jesus for them. Don't take that lightly. Happy Thanksgiving!

God, train my thoughts and speech to be grateful so I reflect the heart and character of Jesus.

GREED

Then he said to them, "Watch out!
Be on your guard against all kinds of greed;
life does not consist in an abundance of possessions."
LUKE 12:15 NIV

Have you ever been shopping on Black Friday? Perhaps you've waited in crowded aisles, hoping to fill your cart with all the newest and hottest items. It's chaos! All to get more stuff at the lowest price. We live in a more-is-better culture: a culture that tells us that if we can just possess the right things, we will be happy and content. But what if our culture is wrong?

The reality is that within the next twelve to twenty-four months, most of what was purchased this year on Black Friday will be broken, tossed out, or useless. How can we instead give gifts that will not lose their value over time? This Christmas, how can you and your loved ones give gifts that help share the true meaning of Christmas with others? Not only will you be sharing the gift of the gospel with others, but you'll also be creating memories. Memories that will last a lifetime.

God, protect me from the greed for stuff. Help me to know my identity as a follower of Christ. Help me this season to share the true meaning of Christmas.

RELATIONSHIP RESTORATION

Do not cast me from your presence
or take your Holy Spirit from me.
Restore to me the joy of your salvation
and grant me a willing spirit, to sustain me.
PSALM 51:11-12 NIV

Can you hear his heart's cry in these verses? Don't send me away. I know I was wrong, but I want to stay in your presence. "Cleanse me from my sin," the psalmist says just a few verses previously (verse 2). He knew that the relationship had been broken.

The psalmist knew there was nothing worse than to be banished from the presence and fellowship of the Lord. But he also knew that the way to restore his relationship was to seek forgiveness, to plead for mercy from a loving God. Today, rest assured that your loving heavenly Father wants you to be in relationship with him as you want to be in relationship with your children.

Father, thank you for Jesus and providing a restored relationship with you no matter what I have done. Restore to me the joy of your salvation. Let me more fully be in relationship with you. Show me where I am unclean and cleanse me.

FAITHFULLY COMMITTED

*Jesus Christ is the same
yesterday, today, and forever.*
HEBREWS 13:8 NLT

Jesus has never left a project unfinished. He has never started a season and quit because he got bored with the sport. His garage is not filled with late-night impulse buys from a home shopping channel that he used once and never came back to. Jesus and his mission are the same yesterday, today, and forever.

Take heart that the Savior still has plans for you. You may not be the new model or the latest craze, but Jesus is still committed to his relationship with you, to fulfilling his plan for your life. He is committed to you!

Jesus, thank you for sticking with me even through my dark days. You have never left me, and you never change your plan for my well-being. May I be faithful to your faithfulness.

AFFIRMATION OF OTHERS

"My command is this:
Love each other as I have loved you."
JOHN 15:12 NIV

It's easy to love others who already love us. It's harder to love others when they are acting like jerks. Yet here the command we are given is to love others as we have been loved. As Jesus spoke to his disciples, they may have remembered being cheating tax collectors and dirty fishermen when Christ began to love them.

Love others as Christ has loved you. Love your coworker who cheated to get the promotion you deserved. Love your neighbor when you step in the present his dog left you. Love one another as Christ has loved you.

Jesus, help me to love the unlovable. Help me to obey you by loving as you loved, by loving those who may not seem like they deserve it. Thank you for loving me as I am.

WORSHIP

Guard your steps when you go to the house of God; to draw near to listen is better than the sacrifice offered by fools; for they do not know how to keep from doing evil. Never be rash with your mouth, nor let your heart be quick to utter a word before God, for God is in heaven, and you upon earth; therefore let your words be few.

ECCLESIASTES 5:1-2 NRSV

We often speak before we think. The proverbial foot-in-mouth disease. Sometimes we catch it just a second or two after our words come out, and sometimes it's days later when we think back to the conversation and realize, Oh, that's why they got mad. The warning here is to keep your foot out of your mouth before God. Are we claiming to be holy as we walk into the house of the God for worship, while we spend our weeks living in unconfessed sin? Are we quick to tell others how they should live and love, while we ignore our own advice?

We serve a God in heaven who knows us completely. There is great freedom in knowing that. There is great comfort knowing that we can enter into worship because God knows us and loves us still. Let us be honest in our worship.

God, help me keep my words few and my worship true, and may my honesty spill forth before you.

ACCESS TO THE THRONE

Since, then, we have a great high priest who has passed through the heavens, Jesus, the Son of God, let us hold fast to our confession. For we do not have a high priest who is unable to sympathize with our weaknesses, but we have one who in every respect has been tested as we are, yet without sin. Let us therefore approach the throne of grace with boldness, so that we may receive mercy and find grace to help in time of need.

HEBREWS 4:14-16 NRSV

We all want special access. Administrative rights, all-access passes, VIP status, or the key to the executive suite. Through Christ Jesus we are given something even better than all these things. We are given access to the throne room of God. We get to walk in like we own the place and can approach the throne of grace with boldness. No fear that we don't belong. No fear that they will find out our credentials are not enough.

The great thing is we are not relying on our credentials but on Christ's. He grants us access to the throne, where we receive mercy and grace right when we need it. All we need to do is enter in and ask. Come on in, access granted.

God, may I be bold in my requests. Thank you, Jesus, for giving me access to the throne room of God. May I stand before the throne in awe but knowing that I belong there because of what you have done.

DECEMBER

Search for the Lord
and for his strength;
continually seek him.

1 Chronicles 16:11 nlt

PIERCING THE HEART

The word of God is living and active, sharper than any two-edged sword, piercing to the division of soul and of spirit, of joints and of marrow, and discerning the thoughts and intentions of the heart.

HEBREWS 4:12 ESV

One of the most difficult things we do as men is try to pass our faith on to others. We often feel inadequate or unprepared, especially when they begin to ask questions and seek to understand God and his redemption story. Yet each of us has access to the most powerful tool for mentoring, the Word of God.

The Word of God penetrates to the heart of the matter. It speaks to intentions of the heart. The better we know it, the easier it becomes to use its insights to pass on wisdom to the people in our lives. A simple word of Scripture can bring to light people's motives, helping us to better talk with them about the things of God.

God, thank you for your Word. Help me to better understand it and its place in mentoring those around me. Allow your Word to wash over me and fill me, so I am full to share with others.

INTEGRITY

"If we are thrown into the blazing furnace, the God whom we serve is able to save us. He will rescue us from your power, Your Majesty. But even if he doesn't, we want to make it clear to you, Your Majesty, that we will never serve your gods or worship the gold statue you have set up."

DANIEL 3:17-18 NLT

Faced with certain death, Shadrach, Meshach, and Abednego stood up to the only person who could have set them free. With a simple word, King Nebuchadnezzar could have shut the furnace off and sent them on their merry way. Yet the three, instead of waffling, doubled down on the God they served. With a certainty that came from walking hand in hand with God, they placed their hope in him alone.

How easy it is for us to compromise to make life easier. The integrity of these three men is amazing. A simple knee taken would have set them free. God would have known their true hearts, and yet they knew that, before God, their integrity would be more important than their lives. We too can have this type of resolve in the face of moral decline around us. Stand firm knowing that God is faithful no matter the circumstances.

God, thank you for the example of integrity of men who have gone before us. Help me to live with honor in every small circumstance as well as every dramatic event.

SUFFICIENCY OF GOD

"I am the Alpha and the Omega," says the Lord God,
who is and who was and who is to come, the Almighty.
REVELATION 1:8 NRSV

Do you often question what the future will bring? Will you still have a job next year? What do your friends really think of you? Why do the ones you love get sick, and will they recover this time?

Whatever questions keep you awake at night, God already had an answer for it. He says to us in our worries and questions, "I am the one who is and who was and is coming." He has seen all time, he is all-powerful, and he knows the answer to your questions. While you stare into the future, wondering what will come, God holds it in his hands and says to you, "I am God All-Powerful!"

God, as my worries surround me and feel like they are overwhelming me, may I rest in you. May I find comfort in you being Alpha, first, and Omega, last. Thank you for knowing and holding the future so I don't have to.

FORGIVENESS

Be kind and loving to each other,
and forgive each other just as God forgave you in Christ.
EPHESIANS 4:32 NCV

Often one of the first thoughts that comes when someone reads this is, But you don't know what they did to me. Or we think that we'll forgive when they ask for forgiveness.

Being kind and loving to one another is something we as men also deal with often. Sometimes we think our love language is sarcasm and snide remarks, as we cut people down with words instead of building them up. Here we are encouraged to forgive, love, and be kind, not as unbearable burdens but as ways to live that will let us be free from bitterness and unforgiveness. Christ forgave our sins on the cross long before we had a chance to seek forgiveness.

Christ, you forgave my sins on the cross, so let me forgive as you forgive. Let my life be filled with kindness and loving others. Help me to speak words of comfort and affirmation to those around me.

CALLED TO PREACH

Those who were scattered went from place to place,
proclaiming the word.
Acts 8:4 nrsv

These first-century believers who fled weren't the leaders of the church. They weren't people we would consider preachers in today's society. They were Spirit-filled followers of Christ. Under threat of persecution and death, these followers shared the love of Christ with those around them.

We are called to preach also. This can start with us sharing the good news of Jesus with our family and then include spreading the news to others around us as we grow deeper in our relationship with Jesus. As we know Jesus more, we can preach his good news more!

Jesus, help me to know you more. Help me to preach your good news to others around me. May I not be afraid to share your love to those in need.

DEVOTION TO JESUS

When they saw the boldness of Peter and John and realized that they were uneducated and ordinary men, they were amazed and recognized them as companions of Jesus.
ACTS 4:13 NRSV

What a compliment! Okay, the words illiterate and uneducated are probably not words you want to be known by, but the leaders marveled at them. Peter and John had silenced those who accused them. They had boldly declared the truth of the gospel to the rulers of the law.

The rulers were amazed, as uneducated men had spoken truth in a way that they could not argue with or contradict. Then came the most beautiful compliment that a Christ follower could ever receive: "They recognized that they had been with Jesus." What a statement! We also want people to see that we have been with Christ.

Jesus, give me the same boldness you gave Peter and John. Remind me to spend time in your presence. May your light shine through me to those who need to hear your truth.

SHELTER AND STRENGTH

God is our refuge and strength,
a very present help in trouble.
Therefore we will not fear, though the earth should change,
though the mountains shake in the heart of the sea;
though its waters roar and foam,
though the mountains tremble with its tumult.
PSALM 46:1-3 NRSV

All around us the world seems to be falling apart. Watching the news, we can feel overwhelmed by the number of heartbreaking things happening around the world. Even closer to home there is pain: families in distress, financial burdens, the death of loved ones, and the list could go on.

The psalmist wasn't writing this psalm in blissful ignorance. He knew the world is full of sorrow, but he held strong to the promise that he had seen, that God is our shelter and strength, always ready to help. In our situation God is there. He wants to help and will help no matter what is happening in or to us. He is our shelter. As the storms rage around us and even on us, he is still there sheltering us.

God, I need your shelter and strength. The pressures of today seem to overwhelm my hope. Reveal your strength, and may my hope not fade even as the world roars around me.

LONGING FOR GOD

As a deer pants for flowing streams,
so pants my soul for you, O God.
My soul thirsts for God, for the living God.
PSALM 42:1-2 ESV

If we're thirsty, we're already partially dehydrated. It's our body's way of telling us we need hydration. We need fluid before our systems start to shut down. Growing up, we quickly realized the signs of thirst. Dry mouth, itchy throat, feeling the need for liquid. When we're thirsty, we drink something.

But what about the soul? Do we know the signs of soul thirst? Do we know the signs of longing for God? Sometimes soul thirst is revealed through a short temper, unkind words to those we love, or feeling far from God. What is the answer to a soul thirst? Time with God. Like a deer who runs full bore to the river to drink, in our times of soul thirst we need to run toward God and let his living waters restore our soul.

God, when my soul thirsts, may it thirst only for you. Help me to recognize the signs of soul thirst and run to your presence. May I long for you and your presence as the deer longs for flowing streams.

TIME WITH GOD

Now more than ever the word about Jesus spread abroad; many crowds would gather to hear him and to be cured of their diseases. But he would withdraw to deserted places and pray.
LUKE 5:15-16 NRSV

Jesus knew he was the one the crowds wanted to see. He knew he was the one who brought healing and hope for the people pressing in around him. Yet in the midst of enormous crowds, faced with all the pressure of healing these people, Jesus retreated to quiet places to pray. He knew the priority of being in right relationship with the Father as he ministered.

As men, the best thing we can do is make sure we're right with God. Sometimes slipping quietly away means setting our alarms earlier than those around us, or staying up just a little bit later to spend time talking with the Father. The best thing a man can do is spend time talking with his heavenly Father.

God, help me to follow the example of Christ. Help me to slip away to be with you. Wake me up to be with you. Keep me up to be with you. May our conversations together be life-giving as I slip quietly away to spend time with my heavenly Father.

ENCOURAGEMENT MATTERS

*Encourage one another and build up each other,
as indeed you are doing.*
1 THESSALONIANS 5:11 NRSV

We have all received at one time or another. A kind word or note brings light into our life. An encouraging word can brighten our day. Encouraging words cause us all to do more together. The Scripture here encourages us to be an encouragement.

So many times it is easy to be critical, thinking that will encourage people to do good. But an encouraging word goes so much further! We can be an encouragement to others simply by telling those close to us what they mean to us. As a man, your words can bring life. Take courage that you can do this!

God, I want to encourage those close to me. Help me to see others around me who might need an encouraging word today. Open my mouth to speak words of encouragement to those who are in need.

SALVATION THROUGH CHRIST

Here is a trustworthy saying that deserves full acceptance:
Christ Jesus came into the world to save sinners—
of whom I am the worst.
1 TIMOTHY 1:15 NIV

This is not something most of us would include in a letter going to our church. But here Paul remembers who he is, thanks to Christ and where he would be without him. Christ came to save sinners. We all need Jesus. We all need to be saved from our sins. This is why Jesus came to earth.

Paul, who gave his approval for murdering those who followed Christ, never forgot from what he was saved. He is no longer living in condemnation. He knew full well that his sin was covered at the cross and that is why he freely said, "Of all the sinners, I am the worst." No matter our past, in Christ we are saved. We too have been saved from death to life and can live in freedom because Christ Jesus came into the world to save sinners—us!

Thank you, Jesus, for your salvation. Thank you for forgiving all my sins. Past, present, and future, my sins are forgiven. Thank you!

INTERCESSION

First of all, then, I urge that supplications, prayers, intercessions, and thanksgivings be made for everyone, for kings and all who are in high positions, so that we may lead a quiet and peaceable life in all godliness and dignity. This is right and is acceptable in the sight of God our Savior, who desires everyone to be saved and to come to the knowledge of the truth.

1 TIMOTHY 2:1-4 NRSV

Our prayer list just got a bit longer. We may be used to praying for those close to us—for our family, friends, and coworkers—but Paul adds a few more people to the list: everyone. That list just became over seven billion names long. And what should we pray? Pray that all will be given the opportunity to be saved and come to a knowledge of the truth.

We have people around us who we know need the Savior's love, but there are also billions of people we don't know who need salvation. One of our roles as a Christ follower is to pray. By praying we enter into the work of God. We are invited to pray for others around the world, not just those close to us. We can ask God to intercede in their lives and reveal himself to them.

God, reveal yourself to those in need of you. I ask that you intercede in their life in powerful ways. May your love be revealed to those both near and far who are in need of your love.

EQUIPPING

Fight the good fight of the faith; take hold of the eternal life, to which you were called and for which you made the good confession in the presence of many witnesses.
1 TIMOTHY 6:12 NRSV

It's not easy. Every day we're faced with opportunities to cheat or lie, to cut corners or to not be men of integrity. This struggle is not something new. Here Paul is equipping his protégé, Timothy, to fight the good fight of faith.

The fight of faith is often internal. We might question our convictions, but we must cling to the salvation to which we were called. We may fight a battle each day to stand our ground in faith but take heart; it's a battle worth fighting.

God, help me to fight the good fight of faith. Help me to cling to the hope of eternal life. As pressure pushes in all around me, may I fight for what is right and true. Thank you for strength to fight.

SAVED BY MERCY

He saved us, not because of the righteous things we had
done, but because of his mercy. He washed away our sins,
giving us a new birth and new life through the Holy Spirit.
TITUS 3:5 NLT

These verses are often hard for us to understand. We're saved not because of anything we have done, but only because of his mercy. As we believe this truth, our faith deepens. If we had done something that could have earned salvation, then it makes sense in our minds that we deserve salvation. We think we can rely on our good deeds or righteous acts to bring salvation, but in Christ's economy our deeds cannot bring salvation. So we must have faith in his promises.

It is this faith that saves us by his mercy. We are then given new birth and life through the Holy Spirit, to live according to the mercy given to us. Our righteous deeds flow out of and not into salvation. We do what is right because of God's mercy given to us and not to earn his favor.

God, increase my faith so I may continue to live in this understanding of how your mercy works. You love me and saved me by your mercy, not because of things I had done. Thank you.

RITES OF PASSAGE

"The LORD bless you and keep you;
the LORD make his face to shine upon you,
and be gracious to you;
the LORD lift up his countenance upon you,
and give you peace."
NUMBERS 6:24-26 NRSV

God instructed Moses to teach Aaron to use these words to bless the people of Israel. Since then, these words have been prayed over people at the end of worship services and repeated often as young people set off on another phase of their journey. They're not just words to be repeated but a prayer of blessing over the people of God.

In the same way, we can pray this blessing over people. God not only hears this prayer but answers it. As we pray it over the people in our lives, we instill in them an understanding of where good comes from. As we ask God to be good to them, we can have conversations with them about where good things come from. This can become a recurring conversation as we talk not only to God but also about God.

God, please bless and protect my loved ones from things that would bring them undo harm. Show them mercy and more kindness than they can even begin to fathom. God, be good, oh so good to them, and give them peace that is real, lasting, and eternal.

PASS THE FAITH

"This may be a sign among you. When your children ask in time to come, 'What do those stones mean to you?' then you shall tell them that the waters of the Jordan were cut off before the ark of the covenant of the LORD."
JOSHUA 4:6-7 ESV

God knew how quickly we would forget. He knew how easy it would be to not share our faith story with future generations. We so quickly forget the amazing things that God has done for us. We forget the financial provision and the healing he has done.

It's important to use reminders to help us pass on our faith to others. Just as God instructed the people of Israel to build memorials, we to can build modern memorials to pass the stories of our faith down to the next generation.

God, remind me of the things you have done in my life. Help me to share these stories with the next generation. When I forget, please bring to mind all you have done.

BOLD FAITH

"Give me this hill country of which the LORD spoke on that day; for you heard on that day how the Anakim were there, with great fortified cities; it may be that the LORD will be with me, and I shall drive them out, as the LORD said."

JOSHUA 14:12 NRSV

Caleb was eighty-five years old at this time. After wandering in the wilderness for forty years and fighting for five years to get to this land he had been promised forty-five years before, he didn't shy away from the battles that still were before him, instead holding to the promise in the Lord.

God is not always looking for the youngest, fastest, or most equipped to do his will. He is looking for people of faith who remember his promises and say, "I will take the hill before me, because God has promised that he would give it to me." Remember God's promises as you face the mountains of your life and trust him to go with you.

God, may I have the faith of Caleb. Help me to remember your promises and trust only in them. May I see your promises and not the battles before me. Help me to be as bold today as Caleb was at eighty-five.

INTEGRITY

When his master heard the words that his wife spoke to him, saying, "This is the way your servant treated me," he became enraged. And Joseph's master took him and put him into the prison, the place where the king's prisoners were confined; he remained there in prison.

GENESIS 39:19-20 NRSV

The world tells us do the right thing because if you do, good things will happen. God says do the right things because it's the right thing to do. Joseph has just stood up to sexual temptation. He has kept his purity, and instead of being rewarded, he was thrown into prison. "And there he stayed," verse 20 concludes. Joseph had done the right thing and yet here he sat in prison.

Even so, the right thing remains the right thing. As men, we want people to see us doing the right thing even if it costs us. Doing the right thing is always the right thing.

God, I pray you would help me to always do the right thing. I want to do right, not to be rewarded for doing right, but because I want to be right in your eyes. Thank you for revealing to me the right thing to do today and each day.

FORGIVENESS

Do not be distressed, or angry with yourselves, because you sold me here; for God sent me before you to preserve life.
GENESIS 45:5 NRSV

Sold as a slave, falsely accused, and thrown in prison. This all happened because Joseph's brothers had hated him. Yet here we see Joseph not only forgiving his brothers for this mistreatment but also asking them to forgive themselves. Imagine how many times Joseph had opportunity to reflect on the wrongs done to him because his brothers hated him. But he did not become bitter. Instead, by the grace of God, he began to see things through God's eyes.

All this happened so he could later save lives. Joseph granted forgiveness to his brothers because he could see that God was in control and had a plan, even for the pain that he endured. The same is true for us. God has a plan for the wrongs that have been done to us, and we need to forgive, knowing that God can yet redeem the pain we have experienced.

Help me to forgive as Joseph forgave. I want to see things in the light of eternity.

DISCIPLINES

"A good man brings good things out of the good stored up in his heart, and an evil man brings evil things out of the evil stored up in his heart. For the mouth speaks what the heart is full of."
LUKE 6:45 NIV

If we want good things to flow from our mouths and into the lives of those around us, we need to spend the time it takes to fill our hearts with good things and empty them of evil. When we confess our sins to God, we empty our hearts to him.

This is a good practice to go through daily with God. Ask him to reveal any evil in you and confess it to him and ask him to replace the evil with his good. Our hearts must be consistently filled with Christ so we can speak good things to our family and friends. Daily Scripture reading helps us to fill our hearts and minds with his Word and good things.

God, I confess to you the evil I have harbored in my heart, and I ask that you fill my heart with you so I may speak right and good words to my loved ones.

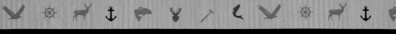

FILLED TO OVERFLOWING

May the God of hope fill you with all joy and peace in believing, so that you may abound in hope by the power of the Holy Spirit.

ROMANS 15:13 NRSV

Hope is contagious. When hope starts to show in someone, it can't be held back from spreading to others. Here the author of Romans prays that we may be filled will all joy and peace so that we may overflow with hope by the power of the Holy Spirit.

We do not have a false sense of hope, joy, or peace; these things come from the God of hope. These things fill us to overflowing. And we don't store hope only for ourselves; it is to overflow to those around us by the power of the Holy Spirit. The hope in us brings hope to others and opens doors for us to share the gospel with those we know.

Lord, fill me to overflowing with hope, joy, and peace. May those around me see the hope I have in you. Guide my heart in peace, bring joy even in sorrow, and give hope to overflowing for those around me.

GOD IS FAITHFUL

*God is faithful; by him you were called into
the fellowship of his Son, Jesus Christ our Lord.*
1 CORINTHIANS 1:9 NRSV

Some guarantees are better than others. There are lifetime guarantees that are only good for a few years, and there are some guarantees that aren't even worth the paper they are written on. The guarantee is only as good as the person or company backing it.

The guarantee given here is one that is worth more than any gold or silver could buy. We will be counted as free from all sin and guilt, because our guarantee is from God himself. And God always does what he says. This guarantee is one we didn't have to purchase; it was given to us through Christ and sealed with the Holy Spirit.

Thank you, God, for keeping your promises. Thank you for being faithful and true to what you say.

GIVING GOOD GIFTS

"You fathers—if your children ask for a fish, do you give them a snake instead? Or if they as for an egg, do you give them a scorpion? Of course not! So if you sinful people know how to give good gifts to your children, how much more will your Father in Heaven give the Holy Spirit to those who ask?"
LUKE 11:11-13 NLT

There is nothing like the face of a child on Christmas morning, especially in that "first see" moment as they come downstairs or turn the corner into the room where the Christmas tree is. The look of pure joy. Fathers love to give gifts to their children, and they will do whatever they can to give them exactly what they ask for. No bait-and-switch or generic gift will do. Giving them what they want is not just indulging a selfish desire on their part; it also indicates that their father has clearly heard them and wants to see them happy, joyful, and fulfilled.

The Father in heaven also knows what is in our best interests: the Holy Spirit. This is the most important gift. As you fondly think of the gifts you received throughout your childhood, remember that these are symbolic of the gifts that the Father has given to us.

God, you know exactly what I need. When I ask for the Holy Spirit, that is what I receive. You do this because you are a good Father who loves to shower his children with what is best for them. Thank you for showing me what good gifts are.

A BIGGER STORY

An angel of the Lord appeared to him in a dream and said, "Joseph son of David, do not be afraid to take Mary home as your wife, because what is conceived in her is from the Holy Spirit."
MATTHEW 1:20 NIV

Even for a carpenter from Nazareth, this was a rough situation. His wife-to-be was pregnant and the baby wasn't his. In fact, his bride claimed that she was found pregnant through the Holy Spirit. He loved Mary, and he didn't want to shame or embarrass her. But his reputation and livelihood was on the line. Joseph was well within his rights to quietly end their relationship.

That's when the angel appeared to him. "Joseph," the angel said, "Don't be afraid to take Mary as your wife." In essence, the angel was reassuring him, "Yes, this is stressful, but there is a much bigger story going on. God is in this, Joseph. God wants you to step up, to love her, to stand with her through everything that is to come, and to accept the joy, salvation, and hope that will come through this child."

God, help me see the bigger reality of Jesus in my life. Let me see the responsibility I have to love and serve those around me, for your sake.

THIS CHILD

"She will give birth to a son, and you are to give him the name Jesus, because he will save his people from their sins."
MATTHEW 1:21 NIV

Imagine trying to raise a child whose birth was announced by angels. Imagine rocking him to sleep, burping him, cleaning him up, playing peek-a-boo, and making silly noises. Imagine his hand wrapped around your finger. Imagine the sound of his measured breathing and the quirky movement of his arms stretched out.

Imagine this child, with the whole world in his hands, entrusted to your calloused, hardworking ones. The responsibility for the one who would shoulder the sins of the world, placed upon the shoulders of this inexpectant father. Joseph was given the incredible privilege and great responsibility to take Jesus as his own. "Jesus," Joseph said. "That's the name I give you. You will be called Jesus, meaning *the Lord saves.*" That's the message of Christmas. This baby, so meek and mild, so full of power, ready to be embraced in your arms.

God, I recommit myself fully to the salvation that comes through the birth of the Savior.

RESTORING OTHERS

If someone is caught in a sin, you who live by the Spirit should restore that person gently. But watch yourselves, or you also may be tempted.

GALATIANS 6:1 NIV

As men, sometimes we're tempted to put people into the place we want them to be. We see them misbehaving and just want to say, "Stop it!" Sometimes we may need to do this when they put themselves into situations where their actions will cause them harm. It is harder, however, to walk gently with them as we see them doing wrong.

We want to force right choices on them. That may work for a time, but it doesn't help them deepen their faith and make the right choices when we're not around. We need to work gently to mentor them in right choices, letting natural consequences take place, as we lovingly help them to understand the importance of their choices.

God, help me to be gentle in mentoring others. Help me to know when to step in and when to step back. Give me patience with them.

POINTING OUT JESUS

The very next day John was there again with two of his disciples as Jesus was walking right past them. John, gazing upon him, pointed to Jesus and said, "Look! There's God's Lamb!" And as soon as John's two disciples heard him, they immediately left John and began to follow a short distance behind Jesus.

JOHN 1:35-37 TPT

John the Baptist really understood what it meant to point people to Christ. Here we see just a brief encounter between two of his followers and him. These two people had agreed to some extent to follow John, to listen to his teaching. They were standing there, perhaps learning from John, when John sees Jesus and says to his followers, "Behold, the Lamb of God!"

Either John didn't know how to stay in business or he knew his role as the one to make the way for the Savior. Our role as men of God is similar to John's: we are to continue to point out Christ, and when our loved ones become his disciples, we let them go and follow him.

God, help me to point out Jesus in the lives of those around me. Help me to release them as they follow you. I want to know you well enough to know when and where you are moving so I can point to you and say to my loved ones, "Behold the Lamb of God!"

FAITH

"Lord, to whom can we go?
You have the words of eternal life."
JOHN 6:68 NRSV

Simon Peter puts his foot in his mouth many times throughout Scripture. He wasn't one to truly think before he spoke. Here, however, he said something that can and should be repeated.

Jesus, after many who were following him left him, asked his closest followers if they too were going to leave. Peter spoke these words and made a confession that has been repeated throughout the ages: "You have the words of eternal life." He had seen it, and we can see it too; Christ's words bring life for eternity. For ages, people have continued to look elsewhere for these words, but they are only found in Jesus.

Jesus, thank you that your words and teachings are much different from any others we have heard. Your words bring eternal life to those who listen and believe. Thank you.

MISSIONS

"You will receive power when the Holy Spirit has come upon you, and you will be my witnesses in Jerusalem and in all Judea and Samaria, and to the end of the earth."

Acts 1:8 ESV

Just before Jesus was taken into heaven before their eyes, he told his followers how things would unfold. The Holy Spirt would come and then they would share his story with all people everywhere.

The Creator and Sustainer of the universe has given us the task of sharing his story with the world. He chooses to involve us and to rely on us to continue to share his story everywhere, including in our own backyards. But the great thing is that we have the Holy Spirit to help us and give us the power to do it.

God, help me to be involved in sharing your story with those all around the world. Help me to lean in to the Holy Spirit and follow his leading to tell the story of Jesus.

UNITY

How very good and pleasant it is
when kindred live together in unity!
Psalm 133:1 nrsv

Often we forget to meet face-to-face with people. Our lives are so filled with texts, e-mails, Skype calls, and Facebook updates that it's easy to forget that we haven't seen our friends in some time. In the verse above, the psalmist agrees that it's good to dwell together.

Dwell is a good word here; it means to spend time together—significant amounts of time, not just the passing "Hey, how's it going?" time together. We need to dwell and converse with others in a way that brings true relationship. Belly laughter, deep connections, and honest pushback and accountability can all be included in the word dwell. It is good to dwell with others in unity.

Heavenly Father, help me to dwell in your presence with others. Help me to be present in the lives of others so we may be blessed by each other and by you.

GOD IS NEAR

The LORD is near to all who call on him,
to all who call on him in truth.
PSALM 145:18 NIV

God is never far off when we call to him. He may seem distant, but God is near. He wants to hear our call, and he wants to answer our call. He never lets our call go to voicemail or asks us to quickly text him because he doesn't have time for us.

He is near to all who call. He is there. Sometimes our perception of him is skewed because of our sin. But he is near. He is always near to us. Reflect on that as you consider the year you have walked through and the new year to come.

God, help me to see how near you are to me. Help me to not feel that you are far off. I want to feel your presence and know that you are here when I call. You have promised you are near, and I want to know you are near.